WRITING YOUR
FIRST PLAY

Stephen Sossaman

Prentice Hall

Upper Saddle River, New Jersey 07458

Library of Congress Cataloging-in-Publication Data

Sossaman, Stephen.
    Writing your first play / phen Sman.
    p. cm.
    Includes index.
    ISBN 0-13-027416-X   nique.   I. Title.
    1. Playwriting.   2. Drama

PN 1661.S67   2000
808.2—dc21   00-038544

Editor in Chief: Leah Jewell
Senior Acquisitions Editor: Carrie Brandon
Editorial Assistant: Sasly Hrasdzira
Managing Editor: Mary Rottino
Production Liaison: Fran Russello/Joan Eurell
Editorial/Production Supervision: Joseph Barron/P. M. Gordon Associates, Inc.
Prepress and Manufacturing Buyer: Mary Ann Gloriande
Interior Design: Circa 86, Inc.
Cover Design: Robert Farrar Wagner
Marketing Manager: Rachel Falk

This book was set in 12/15 Adobe Garamond by DM Cradle Associates, Inc.,
and was printed and bound by Courier Companies, Inc.
The cover was printed by Phoenix Color Corp.

 Prentice Hall

© 2001 by Prentice-Hall, Inc.
A Division of Pearson Education
Upper Saddle River, New Jersey 07458

Printed in the United States of America
10 9 8 7 6 5 4 3 2 1

ISBN 0-13-027416-X

Prentice-Hall International (UK) Limited, London
Prentice-Hall of Australia Pty. Limited, Sydney
Prentice-Hall Canada Inc., Toronto
Prentice-Hall Hispanoamericana, S.A., Mexico
Prentice-Hall of India Private Limited, New Delhi
Prentice-Hall of Japan, Inc., Tokyo
Pearson Education Asia Pte. Ltd., Singapore
Editora Prentice-Hall do Brasil, Ltda., Rio de Janeiro

To everyone rendered mute and inglorious
in the Second Indochina War

CONTENTS

INTRODUCTION

This book will guide you, step by step, to the completion of your first play, from selecting an idea to doing critical revisions, saving you from the frustrating errors that typically plague first-time playwrights. When you have finished, you will have a naturalistic drama ready for play development and perhaps production.

The emphasis is on being practical, efficient, and accessible for beginners. This book has been tested in classrooms with students of varying degrees of theater experience, and it works.

Format and design

Unlike other playwriting texts, *Writing Your First Play* concentrates on fundamental principles, clearly stated. You do not have to wade through a thick text and chatty, discursive paragraphs to discover what you need to know.

This format also makes the text very accessible as a reference guide, since you can quickly reread a critical section.

Exercises and workbook pages

The exercises here focus on you and *your* play in progress, not on a dozen classic plays with which you might or might not be familiar.

Writing Your First Play assumes that you will be writing a one-act or full-length naturalistic drama. This workbook emphasizes the character-centered play, not one driven by plot. This is the best way to become comfortable with the general principles of playwriting before venturing on to more experimental work.

THE BEGINNING
PLAYWRIGHT

ARE THERE RULES FOR PLAYWRITING?

✔ Conventions are important in theater

Conventions are traditions and practices, artistic suspensions of real life. One convention, for example, is that a character whispering to a second character at one end of the stage cannot be heard at the other end of the stage, even though in reality the whisper is loud enough to be heard in the last row.

As Western theater evolved over centuries, theater companies and playwrights discovered what worked, which devices audiences would accept within the illusion of theater. As a new playwright, you would be wise to respect these conventions, and learn to use them.

Your audience knows the conventions quite well. They bring with them a set of expectations as well as hopes.

✔ But you can break the rules

Conventions aren't *rules*, anyway, just practices that have proven successful. Theater evolves when playwrights and others break rules or try new practices to achieve a particular effect or to exploit a new possibility.

Some of those changes are bold, others subtle. Some work well, others fail. Some become conventions themselves, only to be challenged in their turn.

✔ If you ignore the principles, do it for a reason

If your play will benefit from your abandoning a convention or traditional principle, do what the play needs. But don't reject a proven principle without understanding the effect of your choice on your play.

> *"I always feel it's not wise to violate rules until you know how to observe them."*
>
> T. S. Eliot

✔ Spend your time and talents wisely

Write about important matters in the spirit of discovery. Write about what's important to you personally. Don't waste your time emulating a television or movie cliché, or choreographing robotic characters through a predictable story. Write to discover.

WHAT IS SPECIAL ABOUT THEATER?

✔ A theater performance is live

There is an immediacy and vitality about theater. Characters are embodied in living human beings, not conjured in a reader's imagination.

Compare this to film, which is a very distancing art form. The greatest techniques of film (such as jump cuts and varying camera angles) differ from our natural perception. We accept the conventions easily enough, and so can feel great emotion while watching a film, but the form is very emotionally distancing compared with live theater.

Consider, too, why nudity in film is commonplace and nudity on stage is rare, controversial, and in some states illegal. A live nude person is far more emotionally powerful than an image.

But you already know well the magic and mystery of live performance, or you would not have decided to write your first play.

✔ A play performance is a direct representation of action

The audience sees the action as it happens without mediation by a narrator. Being present at momentous happenings can be electrifying.

Theater necessarily uses direct presentation, regardless of whether the approach is realistic or stylized.

✔ Each performance is ephemeral

Each production is different from all the others, and once it is over it is *lost*. Of course, reader-centered theories of literature suggest that the same is true every time a reader finishes a novel or poem.

> *Greek theater is thought to have begun when an orator stopped telling about an event in the distant past, and began to act as if the audience were witnessing that event as it happened.*

Even a videotape or film of a play production does not fully preserve it, although it can document acting styles and the director's decisions.

Friday night audiences are different from Saturday night audiences (usually sleepier), and not all Friday night audiences are the same. Ask an actor about the wide variation among audiences. Actors are very sensitive to slight nuances, even if they can't readily put their perceptions into words.

Actors do not mechanically reproduce the same performance every time. They respond to the audience, get the flu, and try out slight changes in performance. Directors often make changes during a play's run, sometimes with the help of the playwright.

The perishability of a play performance might seem lamentable, but it is an important part of the magic of theater. The excitement and expectation as the curtain rises cannot be matched by cinema.

✔ Each production is collaborative

You are writing the *script*. It takes lots of other people to make this into a *play*. Collaboration means that you are not in control of the final work. No one person is in control, really, although the director tries hard. Many directors won't even want you around during rehearsals, as you might actually interfere with her or his vision of your work by mentioning your own.

Poets would be horrified at losing control over their art, and there are few literary journal editors who would suggest changes to poems they want to publish. Many fiction writers resist their editors' suggestions, but don't expect to find any published novelist who has not made changes, perhaps major ones, at the suggestion or insistence of an editor.

But playwrights know that not having complete control over the play is not only inevitable, it can be very good.

Directors, designers, actors, and others can bring talents and visions to your work that you could not provide. If you don't accept this idea now, you will when one of your plays is powerfully enriched by a fine actor, set designer, or director.

Once the curtain goes up, the audience will be focusing on the actor, not your character. An audience might very well leave a theater praising your play but thinking and speaking only of the actors and the director.

✔ The audience is in a group

Individuals in an audience react to each other. We lose some of our individuality in an audience, a far different experience than we have when we read a poem alone. Laughter is especially infectious, but you've also had the profound experience of knowing that everyone around you in a darkened theater was feeling the same dread or exultation that you were feeling, and this communion with them was probably pleasing.

We all know some people whose laughter makes everyone around them laugh. Hire those people to be in the audience when your comedy debuts! Some theater groups have seated extroverted friends in the row behind the reviewers' seats, so that the reviewers cannot miss their laughter, their wild applause, and their extravagant compliments as they rise for intermission.

Interaction within a group is one reason why the live audience at a comedy club can roar with laughter at a mediocre standup comic. Meanwhile, you can watch the same performance on cable television and wonder how that live audience could think the material is funny. But *they* aren't in a brightly lit living room, alone, drinking fruit juice.

Being in a group heightens the ritualistic aspect of theater, too. There can be a sense of ritual importance to otherwise banal actions.

Being in a group can alter our responses to a work in other ways. In a group we are more likely to feel uncomfortable with overt sexuality, insensitive humor, or descriptions of cruelty. Some people are discomforted by certain subjects and language when they are in mixed company, no matter how they behave with their own sex. If your purpose is *not* to shock or discomfort, keep this double standard in mind.

Each generation complains that the next uses foul language inappropriately. Your senior citizen audience might be strongly repelled if your ingenue protagonist uses profanity or obscenity—well, *you* can think of a word or two that might bother them.

Finally, some audience members may resist responding emotionally to some of your play's most moving moments because they feel very self-conscious about those tears in their eyes. That's *their* problem. Think of them as a challenge, not a hindrance.

✔ Play performances are concentrated

Plays are concentrated in *time* and concentrated in the audience's *attention*.

Except for intermission, there are no interruptions. The performance propels itself forward with no *pause* button and no *rewind* mechanism and no opportunity to turn back pages to reread a confusing passage. One can put a novel down after a chapter, and the phone might ring even if you're in the middle of a poem.

Performances are also concentrated in that they are nearly entirely isolated from distractions. Audiences give performances close attention, but poets never know whether someone will be reading their best poem on the bus, next to a boom box, while watching for her stop, wearing headphones.

In the theater, the lights are down and street noises are muffled or blocked. The stage lighting, action, and dialog dominate. Of course, this extreme concentration means that there is no such thing as a minor cough.

Your story and dialog should easily override minor audience noises. Even if they do not always succeed, audiences are usually self-policing, reproving snorers with elbows and discouraging coughers by a partial glance or by a very slight shifting in their seats (a demonstration of the power of body language).

Theater Isn't Film

Beginning writers, drowned in a film-and-television culture, often make fatal mistakes in writing plays because they do not adequately consider the difference between live theater and television or cinema.

Avoid the common mistakes made by beginning playwrights who are thinking cinematically:

✘ Avoid brief scenes

The camera's ability to jump cut allows filmmakers to use a series of brief scenes, but this is death on stage. Set changes alone make it impractical. Unlike cinema or television viewers, your audience needs time to get involved in a scene. A stage scene must be sustained longer than a film scene.

✗ Don't include difficult actions

Obviously, you won't want to try automobile chases, airplane explosions, or cavalry charges, at least not realistically. Less dramatic actions can create problems, too. Try to avoid writing in fistfights, for example, which are difficult to choreograph and which undermine verisimilitude on stage. Write no parts for children or animals.

✗ Don't rely on irrelevant action

Television programs are filled with physical action to avoid the stasis of talking heads, and that action is not always relevant to the story line. All of the action in your play, on the other hand, should be relevant.

✗ Don't include anything requiring a close-up

Film can provide close-ups in which the audience is made able to see—sometimes *forced* to see—small details, such as the writing on a note or a ring on someone's hand. Your audience cannot zoom in to see details.

By showing a close-up, film can direct its audience's attention to a small action, such as a character surreptitiously pocketing some silverware in a crowded room.

Presented with a close-up, the audience has no choice but to watch that particular action. Your play's audience, on the other hand, cannot be expected to notice such a small action, because they have the ability to move their gaze to other parts of the stage (this is one reason why actors are trained to be still while another actor is delivering an important bit of dialog).

✔ Consider the potential for multiple times and places

Different parts of the stage can represent different locales and different times, one still hovering in the audience's consciousness as a character enters another.

". . . the screen is time-bound and earth-bound compared to the stage, if only because its preponderant emphasis is on the visual image, which, however rapidly it may be changed before our eyes, still displaces its predecessor, while scene-changing with words is instantaneous; and because of the flexibility of language, especially of English, a preceding image can be kept alive through the image that succeeds it. The movie's tendency is always to wipe out what has gone before, and it is thus in constant danger of transforming the dramatic into narrative."

ARTHUR MILLER

Theaters' Requirements

The limited interests and abilities of various theater groups should not overly restrict *how* you write your play, just how you go about getting it produced later. Write your play as it needs to be written, and *then* you can discover which theaters want that sort of play.

When a theater considers your play, it must work within its limitations. To avoid wasting time on scripts they cannot possibly produce, most theaters are quite clear about their interests and limitations in their entries in *The Playwright's Companion, Dramatists Sourcebook,* and other directories.

✔ Technical limitations

Most theaters do not have the machinery, equipment, budget, time, interest, or experience to produce the special-effects theater favored on Broadway. Limitations of space, equipment, and money prevent most theaters from using exotic lighting, multiple scene changes, rotating stages, or elaborate props.

Successful Broadway plays without glitz are rare, but even rarer is the small theater company able to invest considerable time and money in trying to do what film does far better. You're not likely to see a regional theater attempt *Cats.* There are other technical restrictions. Fire marshals frown on open flames, for example.

All art is affected by technological capabilities and limitations. Before long-playing 33 rpm records, jazz groups were limited to recording three-minute songs. Before FM radio was introduced, pop music was mixed to emphasize high and low notes because AM radio could not reproduce the midrange well. Early movies were filmed in black and white because color was not available. Italian Renaissance fresco painters could not achieve the scrupulous detail of Flemish oil painters because their plaster dried too quickly. You get the point.

Does your play require frequent changing of elaborate sets? Moving platforms? A Zeppelin exploding over the audience? A cavalry charge? I hope not. Theater illusion can create any of these effects, but not every theater group wants to.

✔ Cast limitations

If you browse through the theater listings in *The Playwright's Companion* or *Dramatists Sourcebook*, you'll see that each theater specifies its cast limitations. Most have a maximum cast size, determined by the availability of actors or the size of the theater group. Some have a minimum, so that more people in the group can have roles—which is why some schools prefer plays with large casts. Never send a play to a theater whose cast requirements are incompatible.

Unlike professional theaters, many community and college theater groups cannot find enough male actors. Even if the group can find enough males, they aren't likely to select a play with no roles for the women in the group.

A few theater companies are entirely made up of older or younger actors. This affects their casting possibilities, and probably influences their thematic interests as well.

Some theater groups have racial limitations. Whatever its interest in the theme, a white suburban theater group is unlikely to attempt a realistic play about African Americans, because of casting difficulties.

Most plays can arguably be cast without regard to race, and powerful theater can come from nontraditional casting (Imagine *To Kill a Mockingbird* with African Americans playing the white roles, and whites in the African American roles). Many theater companies, especially in colleges, have done similar reversals by casting women in men's roles.

Theater companies interested in such experiments are likely to choose classic plays.

✔ Values and belief systems

Sure, great theater transcends a particular time and place, but that does not mean that theater groups are open to anything.

Theater companies often have explicit or implicit values, political ideas, or social assumptions—and they won't produce your play if it offends their beliefs, or if they think it will offend their audience.

Many regional theaters could not survive without direct or indirect subsidies from local businesses. Companies give grants, provide in-kind services, provide board members with business acumen, buy program advertisements, and purchase blocks of tickets for employees and clients.

A theater that cannot survive without corporations or upscale professionals buying tickets is unlikely to produce an exposé of corporate greed, a revolutionary manifesto, or an attack on suburban hypocrisy. It might not be very keen on a celebration of whatever that community considers radical, obscene, insulting, threatening, antisocial, or immoral.

Many community theaters, even though they do not depend financially on being inoffensive, want only happy plays for happy audiences. That's because happy audiences subscribe for the next year and tell their friends about the theater.

If your play might shock the audience that supports a particular theater, send it to a different theater. A few theater companies only want to do what is shocking, counterculture, eccentric, or challenging.

Some theater companies only want plays that illuminate a particular sort of experience. Check the index to *Dramatists Sourcebook* if your play is likely to appeal to a particular interest. Some theaters seek plays about and for seniors, Christians, lesbians, conservatives, Hispanics, the environmentally conscious, urbanites, children, tourists, or native Americans.

While we playwrights might criticize as provincial any restrictions on our subjects and themes, we should remember that nearly all playwrights have faced this limitation. The ancient Greeks did not put on any pro-Persian plays, and Shakespeare would not have had many Globe gigs if his plays pandered to French nationalism rather than English.

Reread *Tartuffe* to see how the great Molière mollified royalty. Despite its shameless flattery of authority, *Tartuffe* is a great play.

✔ Legal limitations

Real marijuana or live sex on stage will draw more attention from local police than from reviewers. In their haste to outlaw strip shows, some state legislatures are considering vaguely worded, sweeping antinudity statutes that do not recognize any differences among strip bars, family nude beaches, and artistic productions.

✔ Traditional lengths

Theaters usually want full length plays to last 90 minutes to two hours. Most full length plays these days have two acts, allowing one intermission during which the theater can make some money in the lobby selling espresso, chardonnay, tote bags, and season tickets.

Theater audiences want a full evening's entertainment for their money, but what constitutes a full evening has changed over the years. Two and one-half hours, including intermission, is probably as long as most contemporary Americans can tolerate for one entertainment, excepting the Super Bowl. Too short an evening, on the other hand, can leave an audience feeling shorted after buying expensive tickets.

One-act plays can last from about 30 minutes to an hour. Theaters interested in one-act plays (there are not many) usually prefer an evening of "related" one-act plays, related by theme or by having all been written by one author.

BEING A PLAYWRIGHT

✔ Observe people

As a playwright, you must be keenly observant of people, perceptive about human psychology, and alert to the human condition, including yours. You should be honestly and courageously introspective. In addition, you should be attentive to the ways in which people express and conceal thoughts, their patterns of speech, their ways of interacting with each other in a variety of situations.

Throughout your day, imagine that the people around you are actors performing someone else's play—which is not too far from what they *are* doing, if you ask Sigmund Freud or Luigi Pirandello. Imagining this allows you more keenly to observe gestures and speech patterns, to notice distinguishing mannerisms and characteristics, and to ferret out subtext. It also will amuse you at boring parties or meetings.

✔ Learn the craft

See plays and read plays. See different productions of the same play, and see excellent productions a second and third time.

Seeing productions of weak scripts should inspire you, because you can do better. Seeing wonderful productions of excellent scripts should inspire you *even more*, by demonstrating the power of theater. Never be intimidated by great writers. Be inspired by them.

Do volunteer work for a local theater. You will write better plays knowing the production process from the inside. Ask to sit in on several rehearsals, especially early ones.

Read reviews, magazine articles, and books about theater. Join the Dramatists Guild. Take an evening college course. Talk theater, and get opinions about your drafts. You will benefit from what others say.

✔ Create first drafts

Doing the first draft of a play requires intuition, freedom, spontaneity, and energy. Let go. Your knowledge of what makes effective theater will help you write, although you probably will not be conscious of it—you will be too busy writing down what your characters are saying.

✔ Revise to turn your draft into a play

Revising uses different parts of the mind. You are more calculating, more controlling, more interested in *craft*. Use the principles in this book, and scrutinize every detail, every line of your play.

✔ Promote your play

Once your play is *really* ready to submit to a theater, you must stop thinking like a writer and start acting like an agent, entrepreneur, and public relations pro.

Even if the artist in you is insecure, the agent in you must be confident and positive about your play. *Don't* apologize for it, and *don't* say that it needs work. If it really needs work, do that work before offering it to a theater.

Getting plays produced is not easy. No matter how brilliant your play is, no one will come looking for it. Getting your play produced will require time, discipline, self-confidence, and persistence.

The good news is that theaters are always looking for good scripts. Most scripts are not worthy of production, so yours, if done well, has less real competition than you might think when you discover how many scripts theater groups and contests receive. A theater group that gets a hundred scripts in the mail every year does not get a hundred *good* ones.

The Writer's Workbook

Done seriously, your writer's workbook will be of inestimable value for both your current play and future plays, stories, or poems. Gather notes and ideas in a three-ring binder, rearranging pages as you like.

Carry a memo pad or loose index cards with you everywhere, so that you can make notes when ideas occur to you, without relying on memory. Later, you can paste those cards or scribbled-on paper napkins into your writer's workbook.

✔ Story ideas

Once you train yourself to observe life as a playwright, you will encounter hundreds of potential story lines as you chat at work, read the newspaper, and meet new people.

✔ Overheard lines

Learn to eavesdrop. Don't be embarrassed about this. After all, that's exactly what your audiences will be doing with your play: eavesdropping on private conversations. This will help you learn—and recreate in your characters—the particular ways in which people of various classes, jobs, and backgrounds speak.

✔ Character sketches

Record brief descriptions of strangers you encounter. Look for the single telling detail, the unique speech mannerism. For each potential character, invent one characteristic and revealing line of dialog.

✔ Gossip

Henry James wrote lengthy novels from brief bits of gossip heard at dinner parties. Gossip reveals what interests people.

✔ Incidents of dramatic irony and subtext

Look for the subtle and unconscious revelations of self that mark everyone's everyday speech.

✔ Images, scenes, locales

Years from now you might want to set a scene in that remarkable apartment or bus station. Do not rely on memory alone. Note especially the revealing details.

Personal Journal

Your personal journal is an extraordinary tool for recording and understanding yourself. Journal writing helps clarify your current feelings. Reading past journals reveals what you thought and felt at a particular time in the past, overriding the inevitable memory revisionism that allows us to avoid facing the truth about ourselves.

Most people are afraid of the truth. Serious playwrights should work to understand and illuminate truths.

Typical personal journal entries include:

- introspective musings
- fragments of memory
- explorations of dilemmas
- letters, never to be mailed, to the living or dead
- cathartic expressions of strong emotion
- statements of belief, values
- plans, promises, predictions
- assessments of current relationships

PERSONAL JOURNAL: SOME STARTING POINTS

Try automatic writing about each of these prompts (automatic writing requires you to not pause during writing to decide what to write next—just write!):

1. For each member of your family, note down one character strength and one character weakness. Include yourself.

2. Write down your deepest secret. Go on, no one will read it but you. Giving your secrets an existence on the page will help you write your plays more freely.

3. Write down a difficult but important question you would like answered about each member of your family, and your closest friends, a question you would never have the audacity to actually ask.

4. Write a letter to someone who died, saying what you would have said or wished you could have said before they died. Write their response (you can do it, and learn from it).

5. Identify two *conflicting* desires or two *inconsistent* beliefs that you have.

6. Have you ever fantasized committing a crime? Which? Why?

7. What about you is least attractive to the opposite sex?

8. Identify the primary way in which you pleased your parents.

9. Identify the primary way in which you disappointed your parents.

10. Identify your greatest regret, or source of remorse.

11. Write a contract with yourself concerning your writing, including dates due, rewards for success, and punishments for slacking off.

12. Recall one important incident in your youth in which you learned a valuable lesson about yourself.

13. Which person has the most incorrect understanding of you, and why?

Was anything too uncomfortable for you to write?

Did you cleverly avoid the blunt truth anywhere?

Did you feel freedom and clarity by writing about serious emotions?

WHERE PLAY IDEAS COME FROM

✔ A situation

Situation is circumstance, without a significant character: *a guy falls in love with his fiancée's sister*. The gossip you carefully collect in your writer's workbook will probably include several odd situations that pique your curiosity. Be wary, though, of trite situations (the stuff of television drama and sitcoms) or situations that focus on physical rather than emotional matters.

✔ A character

An intriguing character is a fine start, so long as you can find an interesting situation that will illuminate that character for your audience. The character is motivated to achieve an important objective, but faces obstacles and complications.

✔ A visual image

You might see, actually or in your mind, a static image, a place, an arrangement of figures. If such an image attracts you, try freely writing to see if characters and a situation emerge.

✔ A social problem or political idea

The *least* promising start for a play is probably an idea or opinion to which you want to convert the audience. Starting with an idea or theme tends to produce contrived stories with two-dimensional characters. Instead of writing about an issue on which you have loud opinions, try writing about an issue or problem that leaves you feeling ambivalent or uncertain. Your play will be better if you explore and discover the new, rather than propagandize about your certainties.

> "The classic preoccupation of the playwright has been with the family."
>
> ERIC BENTLEY

"Central concerns in all drama are certainly the need to be happy, the inability to face reality, the need not to be humiliated . . ."

JOHN GUARE

"Most great drama is about betrayal of one sort or another."

DAVID MAMET

Situation

An interesting situation is dynamic, not static

There is an uneasy balance, but no stasis. Which would you rather see in a play?

(a) an unhappy wife resigned to her fate

(b) an unhappy wife delivering an ultimatum

A theatrical situation involves conflict

Would you rather see a play about a couple . . .

(a) joyfully agreeing to have a child

(b) bitterly disagreeing about whether to have a child

An intriguing situation pressures characters into choices

Which situation would an intelligent theater audience prefer?

(a) a man cornered by an armed psychopath high on crack

(b) a man forced to choose between keeping his excellent job and keeping his integrity

A promising situation has no predictable ending

The audience wants the outcome to be determined by the characters, who make choices according to their wants and fears, their strengths and their weaknesses.

SITUATIONS

Write three situations (perhaps from your writer's workbook)

1. _____

   _____

   _____

   _____

   _____

2. _____

   _____

   _____

   _____

   _____

3. _____

   _____

   _____

   _____

Story

✔ **Whatever its source, a play idea always becomes a story**

> *"Some writers see situation first, and others character, but sooner or later all must come to some story."*
>
> G.P. BAKER

✔ **A story has four essential elements**

1. An interesting central character who . . .

2. . . . is motivated to achieve an important objective but . . .

3. . . . encounters obstacles and complications until . . .

4. . . . she or he succeeds or fails.

> *"In every effective play somebody wants something badly. An obstacle comes between this person and the thing that he desires. He struggles with the obstacle and either overcomes it or is overcome by it."*
>
> BRANDER MATTHEWS

> *"A play is the revelation of a character in crisis."*
>
> WELLS ROOT

THE PLAYWRIGHT'S TOOLBOX

CHARACTERS

Character and story are intimately connected, of course. The story is created by what the characters do, but at the same time characters (like real people) are shaped and influenced by what happens to them.

Screenwriters sometimes characterize a movie as either "plot driven" or "character driven." You should look for a balance, of course, but always keep in mind that the most powerful plays rely more on memorable characters and their dialog than on story.

☑ People in life are already "characters"

We understand real people based on what they say and do, the same way we understand characters in a play or film. Each has motives and objectives, some hidden.

If you are worried about creating characters, thinking of real people this way should help you.

☑ Characters have major and minor characteristics

Henrik Ibsen referred to the "fundamental traits and little peculiarities" of characters. Each of your characters will probably have a dominant characteristic or personality trait, and minor ones as well. These combinations transform two-dimensional, flat characters into convincing, round characters.

✔ Our opinion of someone differs from that person's opinion of herself

Do most people fully recognize their faults and weaknesses? Not the ones I know. If your characters are to be realistic, their dialog should probably reveal a self-image that is more flattering and forgiving than the judgment of others. Make sure that your characters have enough egotism, vanity, and self-delusion to make them seem real!

✔ A person's character does not change, but values and beliefs can

Like an alcoholic who quits drinking but remains an alcoholic, a character can try to overcome a fundamental characteristic, but is unlikely to eliminate it. Consider the great tragic heroes, none of whom is able to eliminate his tragic flaw, even though they must come to *understand* that flaw. Your play will not seem quite convincing if your miser is transformed into a happy and generous giver; a generous giver, maybe, but that giving will probably still hurt the miserly part of his or her personality.

✔ We learn the most about people in crises

✔ Secret lives are more interesting than trivialities of daily life

✔ The best characters are not simple

Like interesting people, interesting characters have some mystery about them, and they have some plausible contradictions. Everyone you know has some contradictions and inconsistencies, perhaps real hypocrisies.

If everyone in your audience absolutely agrees about a character, you have probably made that character too simple. If your characters are reasonably complex, your audience is likely to have mixed feelings about them.

Consider this: when we dismiss someone in real life because of a single characteristic ("I don't like Reginald, he's such a snob"), that person no longer interests us.

✔ People and characters are not very interesting once the mystery is gone

Remember that new friend who was *so* exciting in the beginning, and remember how eager you were to learn everything? An effective character should excite your audience that way, so they want to know more.

Do you remember how bored you became with some people once you knew everything? Try not to create characters like that.

> *"Your characters must constantly be capable of surprising you, even when you think you know them well."*
>
> ANDREW HORTON

> *"Approach character as a question rather than as a statement."*
>
> ANDREW HORTON

Major Characters

Your protagonist and other major characters should have all of these qualities. Minor characters should have as many as possible.

Interesting

Stereotypes are not interesting. The *unique* is interesting. The *unusual* is interesting. Uncommon combinations of interests and ideas are interesting. Combinations of strengths and weaknesses are interesting. Contradictions and inconsistencies, if plausible, are interesting.

✔ Motivated to achieve a major objective

Each character has a major objective in your play, and a particular objective in every scene. Everything the character does and says is done towards that objective. Even minor characters have objectives.

> *"Often [a character's] conscious and subconscious goals are in opposition to one another—a woman shutting herself off from the world, when what she really wants is to be loved. Such dichotomies enhance and create complexity in a character."*
>
> LINDA STUART

✔ Dynamic (not static)

The protagonist, at least, undergoes some fundamental change. Your protagonist should undergo a change in understanding and awareness. She or he might also undergo a change in life circumstance (like dying), but a change in circumstance without a change in awareness is a television triviality. Characters who change in significant ways are *dynamic*. Characters who do not change are *static*.

✔ Active (not passive)

Audiences want to follow a protagonist who is *active* in her or his pursuit of an objective, *actively* struggling against complications, even if that action fails. Even minor characters act in pursuit of their objectives. Characters who take no serious action are *passive*.

✔ Round (not flat)

Round characters, novelist E. M. Forster tells us, are psychologically convincing. *Flat* characters are stereotypes or blanks. Great writers like Charles Dickens are able to create a memorable, round character with a single descriptive characteristic. You can do the same with a single line of dialog, with a little help from the actor.

✔ Unique in the play

If your play has three elderly Episcopal ministers from Indiana, be sure each is unique—and none is stereotypical. Every juror in the screenplay *Twelve Angry Men* is unique.

✔ Responsive to other characters

Your director will ensure that the actors are constantly connecting with and responding to each other on stage, not just delivering their own lines. To make their jobs easier, your dialog should ensure that your characters do the same.

Of course, there might be a scene in your play in which one character ignores or misunderstands another, is only half paying attention, or is so self-involved that she or he is not really responding to what the other says. At times certain characters' dialog might appear disjointed, marked by non sequiturs, spoken at cross purposes.

✔ Consistent

Characters should not go through unexplained, abrupt changes in their attitudes towards others, their values, or their personalities. One of the values of asking actors to do a reading of your play is that each actor will notice any problems of inconsistency (a kind of continuity) that you might not have noticed on your own.

✔ Plausible

Without creating stereotypes, be sure that your characters are plausible. A church deacon is unlikely to use coarse language and the sweet old librarian would probably not be the town's major drug dealer.

✔ Sane

Avoid the cheap trick of some mystery writers, whose murderer sometimes turns out to be the nice old lady who has no plausible motive, but is just crazy. If you can justify a major character's actions only by revealing insanity, you have failed your audience, and they will know it.

Stereotypes are likely to be more successful in comedy or satire than in drama.

Protagonist and Antagonist

✔ Your protagonist

The protagonist is your central character, whose struggle to meet her or his objective is of the greatest interest and importance to your audience.

The protagonist does not *have* to be sympathetic, although it usually helps. The protagonist *does* have to be interesting.

Your protagonist might represent an entire class of people you find interesting (perhaps battered women or disillusioned artists), but she or he must *first* be a convincing individual. Audiences are not as interested in a whole class of humanity as they are in an individual they have come to care about.

You are not writing shallow genre novels, like romances and men's adventure pulp. Your audience does *not* have to identify with and admire the protagonist, just find her or him interesting, and care about the outcome of your protagonist's struggle to overcome the obstacles to an important goal.

✔ Your antagonist

The antagonist is the character who stands in the way of your protagonist. Some plays have more than one antagonist, but focusing on one is usually best.

The antagonist does not have to be unsympathetic, just in the way. In a romance, for example, the antagonist might be a charming, but reluctant, woman being courted by the charming protagonist; in this case, the antagonist is so very likable that the audience is eager to have her marry the protagonist.

Perhaps your protagonist is opposed by some very large force (such as religious intolerance, corporate greed, racism, or male chauvinism). Find an individual character to represent this force.

Levels of Motivation

✔ Every character has a major objective

The character knows what it is, and considers it very important. In television action movies or blockbuster bestsellers, the objective is usually overtly dramatic—preventing a war, or stopping an assassination, or thwarting terrorists.

In your play, the character's major objective might be less dramatic, but more important emotionally—perhaps reconciling with an estranged parent, or establishing independence, or understanding the past.

✔ Every character has minor objectives, too

These might be created or resolved during the play. Some will directly relate to the major objective. A character might want to get through law school as a minor objective necessary to achieve a major objective: impressing his father or proving his worth to himself.

✔ A character might not fully understand her or his own motives

Ask Freud. A character might be very clear about an objective, but wrong about *why* that objective matters. Your audience will be pleased if it feels that it understands a character better than that character understands herself. This superior insight is one of the great pleasures of great theater.

✔ A character might come to understand her own motives, finally

Classic plays often have as their most powerful moment *the recognition scene*, in which the protagonist finally understands what we in the audience have known, perhaps in pity and horror, for some time. The protagonist's recognition might be *your* play's most powerful moment, too.

✔ Motivation can have more than one level

Everyone *thinks* that she knows why she wants and does certain things. We have at least the illusion of making rational decisions based on proper motives that don't embarrass us.

On the other hand, a commonplace of psychology this century is the belief that in actuality we make decisions and set goals based on emotions we do not fully understand, on subconscious fears and desires.

As a playwright, you will want to exploit this fundamental, often painful, condition.

✔ Backstory can clarify a character's motivations

Screenwriters use *backstory* to refer to the backgrounds of characters and the events that occur before the opening of the film. Some writers construct elaborate biographies of their main characters to better understand how those characters will think, act, and react. Most of the facts of the backstory will never appear in the screenplay, but they are a tool for the writer.

If one of your characters is too mechanical or shallow, consider writing her backstory. Know what kind of childhood she had, where she went to school, whether her parents were strict or indulgent, what her political and religious feelings are. If you *know* that her family lived in shabby genteel poverty, her reactions to issues of money and social status and shame might be clearer to you, and more convincing to your audience, even if the audience never learns about her impoverished youth.

LEVELS OF MOTIVATION

Here is a fine device for increasing your awareness of varying levels of motivations, and for achieving greater introspection.

Why do you want to write a play?

Answer by finishing this sentence: "I want . . ." Ask yourself why *that* answer is true, and answer again, using the "I want" form. Keep doing this until you can go no further.

If you do this for three or four rounds, and answer *honestly* enough, you will probably get to some human fundamental: love, security, admiration, compensation for some loss, self image, eliminating shame, self-actualization.

Consider this imaginary example:

Q: Why do you want that new job, John?
A: I want to make more money.
Q: Why?
A: I want to drive a better car.
Q: Why?
A: I want women to want to date me.
Q: Why?
A: I want my social life to improve.
Q: Why?
A: I want more sex.
Q: Why?
A: I am insecure about my manhood.

Is this far enough? We have gone from an immediate objective to a deeper objective, one that probably will not be mentioned in the job interview.

If we went further with these questions, we might discover that what John *really* wants is to avenge a rejection, compensate for a failure, prove his father wrong, impress his brother, or resist death.

CHARACTER

For each situation on page 19, describe a likely major character, and identify her or his primary motivation.

1. _____

_____

_____

_____

2. _____

_____

_____

_____

_____

3. _____

_____

_____

_____

_____

Treating Characters as Individuals

✔ Treat each character fairly

Write from within the character, not from without. Even a person you despise probably thinks well of himself, and has friends. The nasty people you know probably think they're rather nice.

Give your least sympathetic characters some good points and reasonable objectives.

✘ Do not model characters entirely on people you know

If you base a character on a real person, and base your story on a situation that person really went through, you risk limiting your play by not being able to break free from what really happened.

To free yourself from the reality of that person, give your character an interesting new set of character strengths and flaws, and maybe a new gender.

✘ Do not write about any person or any type you detest

Unless you can *truly* rise above your loathing to create a round character with some redeeming qualities, you will have an uninteresting character.

> *"The best scenes are 'Why are those two people arguing and why are they both right?'"*
>
> NORMAN LEAR

MOTIVATION

1. Identify a friend who is seriously pursuing an objective, and speculate on two or three possible levels of motivation (at least one of which your friend would not realize).

2. Consider the several rewards of your job (perhaps salary, title, praise, sense of accomplishment, chance for creativity, learning opportunity, chance to manage others, interesting challenge, playing a role in providing a useful product or service, etc.). Which of these are most important to you—and why?

3. Be honest: identify one instance in which you did a good deed for a hidden, selfish reason.

4. Identify instances in which you talked someone into something, minor or major, by considering what motivates her or him and what her or his objectives were.

5. Compare your major objectives with those of your significant other. Are they compatible?

6. For each of several friends, complete this sentence (as if she or he wrote it) with her or his major conscious objective: "I want to…"

> *Actors are often taught to prepare for a play by identifying their character's superobjective, her or his most fundamental goal or purpose. Students of Stanislavsky were taught to find an active verb that identifies this superobjective and each scene's objective (for example, "I want to make her distrust Bill."). The actor can then go through the script tracing a through line of action: the various moments leading, one after another, towards the superobjective. What active verb applies to each of your characters in each of your scenes?*

Minor Characters

Try to have no characters so minor that they can easily be eliminated. Sometimes two or three minor characters can be combined into one. (Do you really need a maid *and* a butler *and* a gardener, each with one line?)

Never create characters who are just props without any dialog, such as other customers in a restaurant. If your setting seems to need a background crowd, move your essential characters to some other place (a park bench? a living room?).

Minor characters can fulfill one or more functions.

✔ Advance the plot

Minor characters accomplish many of the minor actions of a play, furthering the development of the plot.

✔ Slow the action to increase suspense

They can also hinder the advance of the plot, but nicely increase tension (for example, by interrupting two shy people who seem about to declare their love for each other).

✔ Be a foil to other characters

A "foil" helps the audience understand a major character by being different (just as the jeweler's dark velvet brings out the hardness and brightness of a diamond). Shakespeare lets his audience better appreciate Desdemona's innocence by showing her with her cynical, immoral maid. Characters can be foils to illuminate other characters' values, not just their personalities.

✔ Justify others talking out loud

Because dialog is the substance of your play, your main characters have to talk to someone so that the audience can overhear. Avoid soliloquies.

☑ Provide comic relief

This probably should not be a character's *only* purpose.

The Audience and Your Characters

☑ Your audience will judge characters as they judge people

They will judge based on what the characters *say and do*, on first impressions modified by the accumulated observations of how they react to events, treat other people, reveal their values, and so on.

☑ Audiences enjoy plausible unresolved contradictions in a character

Iago and Willy Loman fascinate audiences in part because they are not easily understood, and therefore cannot be easily dismissed as uninteresting.

Think about how boring most television characters are, lacking contradictions and enigmas. Is there anything fascinating about the latest television detective? Are there tantalizing suggestions of wonderful psychological revelations to come about in any characters in an episodic show?

☑ Audiences prefer their own opinions, not others'

Do not rely solely on one character's describing a second to illuminate the second. In life, we prefer to judge people on what we see them say and do. We do not easily accept a third person's opinion once we have met and observed the subject directly. In fact, we might learn more about the character doing the talking than about the character being discussed.

PLAY STRUCTURE

✔ The playwright translates story into plot

A story is an amorphous series of connected events, the raw material from which the playwright (like the novelist) selects a few to create plot.

✔ Plot is a series of events connected by cause-and-effect relationships

Events outside of your characters' lives and actions may also occur, but your plot requires that your characters' actions and words have effects. One effect then becomes the cause of another effect.

✔ A play has both a suspense plot and an emotional plot

What we usually think of as the plot is known by some as the *suspense* plot. Here are the events and the dramatic question.

> *"I know for a fact that the only reason one watches something for more than 15 or 20 minutes is because it has a plot and you're curious to know what happens next."*
>
> WALLACE SHAWN

The play's suspense plot keeps the audience attentive while the playwright spends most of her or his time developing the *emotional plot*, which is the heart of the play. The emotional plot explores human nature and the human condition, as revealed through the pressure of the suspense plot.

✔ Some plays have subplots, too

A subplot is an optional secondary line of events, with its own cause-and-effect relationships. The subplot should be related thematically to your main plot. **See page 40**

✔ Plot includes events that do not happen on stage

You must decide which events are worth showing on stage. If an event is necessary to the plot, but not intrinsically interesting, include news of it in exposition, but don't show it on stage.

✔ The resolution arises from character

Resolution should not be imposed externally, or by accident, or by the introduction of any new character or fact at the last minute. (Avoid relying on a *deus ex machina*: any contrived, last-minute device to rescue the playwright.)

Elements of Plot

✔ An inciting incident

This event triggers your play. The inciting incident usually happens before the first action of the play, or in the first scene. The inciting incident upsets whatever balance or stasis might have existed.

In planning your play, always ask why you are selecting *this* moment in the main character's life. The answer is probably that an important inciting incident has happened.

King Lear has led a long and probably boring life. Shakespeare opens his play at the moment when the king announces a really bad retirement decision, which is about to trigger catastrophic results.

✔ An opening

Choose a late point of attack, opening in the middle of the story *(in medias res),* not at the very beginning. Background events can be referred to in exposition.

"By taking our dramatis personae [characters] and precipitating them, in the very first scene, into the highest pitch of their conflicts we turn to the well-known patterns of classic tragedy, which always seizes upon the action at the very moment it is headed for catastrophe."

JEAN-PAUL SARTRE

✔ A dramatic question

The dramatic question is the primary question the audience wants answered. It involves whether or not the protagonist will achieve her or his primary objective, or fail.

✔ Rising action

In the play's *action*, one event leads to another, moving the play ever closer towards resolution of the dramatic question. *Suspense* builds as the audience gets closer to having its curiosity about the dramatic question satisfied.

One of your most critical accomplishments will be setting the pace of this rising action, fast enough to maintain audience interest, and slow enough to build suspense.

✔ Complications

Complications are those detours and impediments that delay and tease us in our eagerness to get to the point.

✔ Crisis

The crisis is the event during which the audience will learn the answer to the dramatic question. In old western movies, the crisis was the showdown between the sheriff and the bad guy as they prepared to draw guns in the middle of the main street.

✔ Climax

The climax is the moment when the audience gets its answer to the dramatic question. In western movies, it's the moment the audience knows whether the sheriff or the bad guy has won the gunfight.

In a full length play, you might find several crises and climaxes, each more powerful than the preceding one, leading to the major crisis. Action-adventure films are little more than a long series of crises and climaxes.

✔ Denouement

Denouement is the brief relaxation of tension after the climax, the falling action. Having seen the dramatic question answered, and ready to go home, your audience needs just a little time to relax physically and emotionally, and emerge from the illusion of your play back into their own realities. If they are moved too fast, they'll get the bends. If you make them sit through too much dialog after the climax, you will destroy the fine effect you labored so hard to achieve.

In many classic plays, a character will step forth to provide some closure, some attempt at guiding the audience's understanding with a philosophic statement or observation. Reread Shakespeare to see this. Modern playwrights avoid this practice.

In mysteries, the denouement is an opportunity for the sleuth to explain how he or she figured out the crime, identifying clues that the audience might have missed.

✔ The end

The end of your play is an especially powerful moment, like the last line of a poem.

You will have resolved the primary dramatic question, but your play can still end on a note of ambiguity about the general fate of the characters.

Audiences want a sense of resolution and closure, but this does not mean that they have to have every little question answered. Some modern playwrights prefer to write *open-ended* plays that end on a note of ambiguity, but unless done very well, open-ended plays can leave an audience feeling unsatisfied, even cheated.

✔ The last line

Your play's last line will especially resonate, and your audience will look for significance there, perhaps an insight into your theme.

Subplots

Subplots, usually involving minor characters, can provide a second line of interest, but are difficult to manage well.

✔ Most one acts don't have subplots

A subplot would probably rob your one-act play of its wonderful unity and compression.

✔ Subplots can enrich full length plays

Consider the extent to which the subplot in *King Lear*, involving Gloucester and his two sons, enriches the play's illumination of parent and child relationships by complementing the depiction of Lear's relationship with his three daughters.

✔ Subplots should parallel or complement the main plot

✔ Subplots can be a comic parallel to the main plot

Elizabethan playwrights sometimes enriched a main plot involving aristocrats wooing with a comic subplot involving servants wooing.

✔ Subplots should be resolved before the main plot

The subplot's dramatic question is less important and less suspenseful than the dramatic question of the main plot. Resolve the lesser question first to increase the suspense about the major question.

Acts

✔ Most contemporary full length plays are in two acts

If your play can be accomplished in less than an hour, make it a one-act play. If it is very long, construct it as three acts.

Contemporary theaters doing classic five-act plays do not impose an intermission after every act. In fact, those five-act plays are often performed as two acts.

A terse one-act play is *far* better than a full length play with pointless filler. Every line of dialog must have a function.

✔ Last acts are almost always shorter than first acts

With some luck, and clever playwriting, your play will have a natural point for the intermission a little more than halfway through. That point will be after a powerful scene.

Deciding where the first act ends might be easy if your play takes place over two days, or at two locations, so long as the relative lengths of the two acts are appropriate.

✔ End your first act with a new cause for curiosity or tension

A new character's entrance immediately before the end of the act helps keep your audience interested during the intermission, as do the act's last lines (the "curtain speech") if they offer a surprise, a new development, or another new cause for tension. Work hard to make your audience at intermission eagerly await the second act, not hurry towards the exit.

Scenes

✔ A new scene is created whenever there is a change of place or time . . .

. . . unless you use various areas of the stage momentarily to represent different places and different times. A character can recall an event in the past, step to a different area, and recreate that event without creating a new scene.

✔ One scene can have several "French scenes"

A "French scene" is created whenever a character enters or exits. Your audience will not think of this as a scene change.

✔ Every entrance or exit changes the dynamics of a scene

What a character says and does depends upon who is present.

Remember back in high school, when you and your date were snuggling on the couch watching television, sort of, and a parent walked in the room? Did you ever have a family argument interrupted, perhaps even silenced, when someone walked by? Use entrances and exits to good effect, and be aware of how the scene dynamics change when someone enters or exits.

✔ Every scene has a plot

Many scenes have a conflict, rising action, crisis, climax, and denouement. Avoid long scenes with no forward movement.

✔ Every character has an objective in every scene

Each character's objective in a scene is probably related to her or his major objective. Sometimes a character can have a series of objectives during a scene. (See Appendix E for a demonstration of how one character in Henrik Ibsen's *A Doll's House* has 15 successive objectives in the last act.)

✔ Scenes can create a play's rhythm

Some playwrights alternate scenes that are densely verbal with scenes having more action, or alternate high tension scenes (conflict and confrontation) with less stressful ones (exposition, romance, or comedy).

A good rhythm can also be created by alternating two-person scenes with scenes having more characters.

✔ Start each scene as late as possible

This is *choosing a late point of attack*. Your audience does not have to see one character enter a room and exchange pleasantries with another before important dialog. Open the scene with the two already past the pleasantries, and start with important dialog.

✔ Many plays have an "obligatory scene"

An obligatory scene (*scene-a-faire*) is the one to which your whole play seems to be leading. Audiences will know what it is, and anticipate it with eagerness and dread. It will be the crisis, and will make the climax happen.

In *Hamlet*, it is obligatory for Hamlet eventually to confront the King, who killed Hamlet's father. In old western movies, the sheriff ultimately had to confront the main villain, after getting by the minor obstacles of nameless hired guns.

You have promised this scene to your audience, you have made them eager for it, and you must deliver.

> *"Never put two people in the same scene who agree with each other."*
>
> LEW HUNTER

Beats

A scene can usually be divided into smaller units known as "beats."

✔ A character's immediate objective can change during a scene

Characters sometimes change their objectives in reaction to what others say or do, in response to news, or after a sudden recognition.

✔ A change in objective creates a new "beat"

A character confronted with her lie can move from banter (to distract the accuser) to denial (to discourage the accuser) to admission (to stymie the accuser) to explanations (to mollify the accuser) to compliments (to win the accuser's forgiveness). The accuser might go through several beats, too, changing objectives from forcing the truth out to winning a concession, and then to establishing a new power balance in the relationship.

✔ Your actors will look for beats

An actor preparing for a role in your play will probably "score" the script to mark each new beat, because the way the character acts and talks will change when the beat changes. Remember, all dialog is spoken in pursuit of an objective. When the objective changes, the delivery will change.

FIVE KEYS TO HOLDING YOUR AUDIENCE

✔ Emotion

Your characters' emotional lives are more important than plot.

✔ Secrets

Revealing your characters' secrets is absolutely essential. Audiences want to experience and understand the secret lives of your main characters, not their public image. After all, your characters' secret lives touch your audience's secret lives.

✔ Conflict, obstacles, and complications

Conflict, too, is absolutely essential, even in a love story or a community theater's heartwarming holiday offerings.

Your protagonist must face obstacles, so that achieving the objective is in doubt. Complications wonderfully enrich the characters' struggles.

✔ Tension and suspense

In a play, *tension* is the pleasingly uncomfortable awareness of conflict, worry about serious and unpleasant things likely to happen. *Suspense* is the pleasingly tantalizing withholding of information the audience is eager to know, mainly what is going to happen.

If your play lacks tension and suspense, you will feel the audience squirming with boredom or irritation, *if* your play is ever produced. You want the audience to eagerly want information and resolution just a *little* faster than your play provides. Tease them, then deliver. You must resolve suspense.

Action

Stasis is impossible. Forward movement towards the climax is necessary, generating increasing tension.

Emotions and Secrets

✔ Emotions are more important than ideas in theater

Your play should reach the deep and authentic emotional life of your audience, not just their minds. The best plays arouse a complex of emotions, not simple ones. Many of those plays evoke painful emotions. The first audiences watching Arthur Miller's *Death of a Salesman* did not applaud when the curtain came down, they wept.

Honor Aristotle by providing your audiences with a powerful cathartic and emotional experience, first arousing and then releasing deep emotions.

Melodramas and television, on the other hand, prefer sensationalism, the superficial, and the obvious, like stories about a mother's anguish when a child is kidnapped.

Do horror films evoke deep emotions?

> *"A play exists to create emotional response in an audience."*
>
> G. P. BAKER

✔ Audiences want to know the characters' deepest secrets

Great plays reveal the deep secrets of their audiences, too.

> *"... the audience should feel not uplifted, not superior, not virtuous, but quite the contrary, humbled. ... Each should be reminded of his own sweet and sour humanity...there should resonate within the audience a sense that the situations depicted obtain also for their lives."*
>
> RICHARD WALTER

Conflict

✔ **The conflict should represent issues larger than the characters**

Without turning your living play into an allegory, you should write so that in addition to seeing an individual character in a specific situation, your audience is watching an enactment of a general, perhaps archetypal, human circumstance. Individuals in the audience want you to illuminate their own lives, their own dilemmas and hopes and failures.

You need a delicate balance. The audience is most immediately concerned with the specific lives of your characters, but those lives resonate with larger implications for the lives of the audience.

✔ **The conflict must be very important to the protagonist**

Otherwise there is no suspense about the outcome of the struggle, because it does matter to the audience. Matters of emotion, relationships, and understanding can be very important.

✔ **Your conflict should engage emotions, not just curiosity**

Your audience is interested in more than just how something works out, for the same reason baseball fans want to experience a game, not just learn the score.

This interest is why people can see a dozen performances of *Hamlet* over the years without being sated. How many times can you sit through a story that operates only at the level of plot curiosity? How many times would you want to see the same episode of a typical police show on television?

Emotional conflict is also more interesting than physical conflict. A sharp tongue is a better stage weapon than a knife.

THREE TYPES OF CONFLICT

There are three types of conflict common in literature. Your play should deeply involve the first two. Either may be more important than the other.

✔ Conflict with other individuals

This is the central conflict of most great plays. Of course, the antagonists usually represent a larger force to some extent (for example, conventional thinking or religious intolerance). Your first play should probably be grounded in your protagonist's conflict with one or two individuals who are unique characters first, and representatives of larger forces only secondarily.

✔ Internal conflicts

Internal conflicts wonderfully enrich major characters. If your character is very determined to reach a specific goal, without any conflicting feelings, you are missing an opportunity to create interest and to illuminate the human condition. Nevertheless, a play based *solely* on internal conflict is likely to bore its audience, if it ever gets an audience. Purely internal conflicts are more suitable for poetry.

✔ Conflict with external nature or large forces

This is more easily accomplished in fiction or film. Narratives built on conflict with external nature tend to be adventures with little concern for character. Consider disaster films and stories of airplane crash survivors struggling out of remote mountains.

If your protagonist is in conflict with a large and amorphous force (perhaps society), create one or more individual characters to represent that force.

Obstacles and Complications

✔ **Obstacles lie between a character and her or his objective**

Much of a play's interest evolves from the protagonist's difficult struggle to get past obstacles and to overcome complications in pursuit of the major objective. In action films, there is little interest other than this struggle against obstacles, even though the obstacles are often as banal and boring as armed villains. In your play, however, the obstacles and complications are probably secondary to your exploration of character.

✔ **Action is not direct, but interrupted or altered by new complications**

Complications increase tension, are interesting in themselves, and provide smaller dramatic questions on the way to answering the major dramatic question. Try for complications that are intrinsic to your characters and situation, arising naturally rather than artificially. Watch your favorite Alfred Hitchcock film to see how a master increases tension through small and large complications.

> *"One of the greatest difficulties for the beginning dramatist, I have found, is in creating enough complications—the play tends to move in too direct a line to its outcome."*
>
> KENNETH ROWE THORPE

✔ **Each complication should be more intense than the previous**

Insure that tension increases rather than decreases as your play approaches the crisis.

CONSIDER A PLAY ABOUT A CHARACTER NAMED JOHN . . .

John wants to marry Jill, an ambitious New York corporate executive. Which of these obstacles and complications would be most interesting?

(a) *John's car won't start.*

A minor, external and temporary obstacle. Irritating, but banal.

(b) *A giant, radioactive millipede is squatting between his apartment and hers.*

The choice of 12-year-old moviegoers, perhaps. But there is no emotion except fear. The conflict is entirely external (there is no apparent internal or interpersonal conflict). There will probably be few opportunities for intriguing dialog with the millipede. Adult audiences want to see John interact with Jill, not with an insect.

(c) *Jill despises John, because of a misunderstanding, and she loves George.*

Well, here is an interesting problem. This story involves a significant obstacle involving emotion. There is interpersonal conflict between John and Jill, who have conflicting objectives. George might be a problem, too. The misunderstanding, a common device in romances, is an interesting complication.

(d) *John also wants to be a celibate priest working with lepers in India.*

This is an interesting internal conflict. By itself, it is not enough, because purely internal conflicts work better in fiction or poetry. Jill has no role in this scenario.

Consider combining (c) and (d) for best effect, so that your play has both *interpersonal* conflict and *internal* conflict, both born out of incompatible objectives.

Tension and Suspense

Suspense is created by a series of complications in the inexorable movement towards resolution of your dramatic question.

✔ Audiences want to know <u>what</u> will happen

Basic curiosity. The first viewing of a narrative creates some curiosity about what will finally happen. Weak plays, films, and novels generally do not get beyond this modest level.

✔ Audiences want to know <u>how</u> it will happen

The outcome might be obvious, but the audience can still enjoy finding out how the end is reached.

In a romantic comedy, we know that the two main characters will fall in love and overcome whatever obstacles and misunderstandings they face. In a mundane television police drama, we know that the detective will arrest the criminal. What is interesting is the *way* these expected events come about, especially when the obstacles seem formidable.

✔ Audiences want to watch something momentous happen

As in tragedies. The ancient Greeks *knew* how the play would end. If Oedipus knew as much as Greek audiences did, he would not have made such momentous mistakes.

Have you seen a nature film showing a snake prepare to strike a frog? You cannot save the frog, but the suspense is terrific because the event is very important to the frog, and because you know something the frog does not. Your own fear of snakes or your own worry about mortality might make the struggle symbolically relevant to you.

UNCERTAINTY AND INEVITABILITY

To achieve suspense, your play should create a sense of *uncertainty* as the play is experienced during the performance. The greatest playwrights also create a sense of *inevitability*, when the play action is considered afterwards.

✔ The conflict begins after the play begins

When the play begins, there is an imbalance, a possibility of conflict. There might also have been an *inciting incident* that took place right before the opening scene. The opening scene is interesting to the audience because it is pregnant with the possibility of conflict. Whether your audience realizes it or not, they anxiously look for the first sign of conflict.

✔ The conflict must be resolved by the end of the play . . .

. . . even if the end of the play creates a new conflict and instability that might be the subject of another play.

> *"When we are dying to know what is coming next, we sit still and pay attention. When we aren't, we don't—we would rather do almost anything than sit still. . . . [inadequate tension] ruins more productions than any other single problem."*
>
> DAVID BALL

Action

Action does not mean just physical movement, as in a film. An action can be something a character says that represents an important change in the story development. In your play, an action is any

- plot movement forward, towards the play's climax
- change in the current equilibrium of the play
- significant shift in a character's understanding or intent

- revelation of a significant fact to the audience
- significant increase in tension

✔ Keep your play moving forward or the audience will be bored

Action maintains audience interest.

✘ Avoid long sections of dialog that stall the play

Your play can stall while characters deliver set speeches or provide lengthy descriptions of offstage events.

✔ Provide symbolic acts

Symbolic acts are actions that reveal a character's thought or emotion. They are especially useful to signal a *change* in understanding or attitude. Always try to have the physical action on stage and your characters' dialog complement and reinforce each other.

✘ Include no action directed only at arousing emotion

This advice from Konstantin Stanislavsky to actors applies to playwrights, too. Every action should contribute toward the plot movement or towards the revelation of character, or both.

WHAT YOUR AUDIENCE SEES AND HEARS

✔ Sets

Your script should require as few set changes as possible. A single set is easiest on the theater. You can characterize your setting (is the living room elegant or shabby?), but leave the decorating details to the set designer and director.

✔ Props, lighting, music, costumes

Identify props (properties) that are specifically needed. Most decisions about the other visual elements will be made by your director.

✔ Dialog

Dialog is the heart of your play.

✔ Stage movement

Your characters must move around and do things with their hands, not just sit. Stage action creates and maintains visual interest and physically reveals characters' objectives, relationships, and moods. All of your characters' movements should reinforce dialog (for example, by moving towards or away from another character, according to the dynamics of the current moment, the current *beat*).

Leave most blocking details to the director. Leave body language decisions to the actor and director.

> *"In drama, the basis of knowledge of what the characters are and what they experience should come directly through dramatic action and speech."*
>
> KENNETH ROWE THORPE

Sets, Props, Lighting, Music, and Costumes

The less demanding your play is on a theater's resources, the more likely it is to be produced. Simplify your requirements when you can without compromising your script.

✔ Try to use one setting for the entire play

✔ A single set can represent multiple rooms, locations, and times

✔ **Specify only essential props**

✔ **Leave lighting decisions to the lighting director**

✔ **Consider royalty problems when specifying music**

If your script calls for specific music, provide it to the theater on an audio cassette. A theater would prefer to not use music on which it must pay a royalty.

Stage Movement

✔ **Let the director make the major stage movement (blocking) decisions**

You should provide basic, not exhaustive, directions.

✔ **Stage movement reinforces dialog**

Just as everything a character *says* is in furtherance of her or his objectives, so is everything that character *does*.

✔ **Movement reveals characters' emotions and relationships**

One character's moving *towards* another can suggest heightened emotion, whether those emotions are positive or negative. One character's moving *away from* another character might suggest withdrawal, disengagement, anger, or fear.

✔ **Stage movement creates visual interest**

What your audience *sees* on stage should not remain static for very long.

✔ Stage movement draws attention to important props

In films a close-up of an object draws it to the viewer's attention. In a stage play, an actor must accomplish this.

✔ Stage movement should reflect beat changes

Stage movement, like dialog, arises out of the character's current objective, and changes when the objective changes. A woman changing from anger to a desire for reconciliation is likely to stop moving away from a second character, and start moving towards him or her. A seated person becoming suddenly angry will probably bolt out of the chair.

✔ Stage locations have different levels of importance and power

For example, the center of the stage has more energy than upstage left or right. Downstage areas are more powerful than upstage areas.

✔ Upstage and downstage movements have different intensities

Obviously, a character moving towards the audience gets increasing attention, as does a person approaching you on the street. Actors have been known to "upstage" others by standing upstage, facing the audience, forcing another actor engaged in dialog to turn away from the audience towards the upstage actor. An actor with his or her back turned loses some audience interest to the actor facing the audience.

✘ Don't have all of your characters sitting down

Sitting drains the visual of tension.

✘ Don't have movement just for the sake of movement

STAGE DIRECTIONS

✔ **Include essential stage directions**

Include entrances and exits, sounds (for example, a car entering the driveway), and major character actions, like walking to a window or picking up a significant prop.

✔ **Omit nonessential stage directions**

Your director will make adjustments anyway, some of which you cannot easily anticipate while writing the play, but which will be obvious when the actors begin to walk through scenes.

✔ **Include only what can be seen or heard**

If your audience cannot see or hear it, omit it. Beginning playwrights sometimes include what characters are thinking.

✖ **Don't call for long periods of inaction and silence**

The audience will leave if they are asked to watch a character stand still to think for more than a few seconds, let alone minutes.

✔ **Use the accepted form**

The sample script in Appendix A shows the proper form. If fussing with the format distracts you from the writing, you can write your play in any fashion, and correct the form later.

DIALOG

✔ **Every line of dialog must have a purpose**

Time limitations and your need to propel the play forward require that there be no empty dialog, no unnecessary words. In life, most talk is idle chatter, but in your play, even apparently idle chatter must have meaning.

✔ All dialog is spoken to advance the speaker's objective

Unlike real people, who often babble aimlessly, your characters know what they want. Everything they say is in furtherance of their objective in that particular beat.

> *"Like everything else in good art, the writing of good dialog involves selecting what is significant and giving it order. The characters of drama are more articulate and self-revealing than people in life."*
>
> KENNETH ROWE THORPE

✔ Dialog should be rich in subtext

Give your audience the pleasure of reading between the lines, detecting nuances, and picking up hints and clues about what characters think and feel. Your audience needs to play this active role, not sit passively while dialog makes everything obvious.

✔ Dialog must be speakable

That means out loud by an actor, not just to the writer's inner ear. An actor at a cold reading will discover unspeakable lines for you, by not being able to read them naturally. Avoid very long sentences and awkward sound repetitions.

Dialog's Nine Major Functions

Each line of dialog should accomplish more than one function. Here are some of what a line of dialog can accomplish. Some of your play's lines of dialog might accomplish four or five of these at the same time!

✔ Advance the plot

Advancing the plot is perhaps the most fundamental purpose of dialog. Avoid long sections of dialog that do not advance the plot, along with whatever else they do. Long *set speeches* and *exposition* (summaries of past action) work against the important forward movement of your play.

✔ Reveal character

The audience will base its judgment and understanding of characters primarily on what they say and do. Your audience is likely to learn as much from subtext and from the way a character speaks, as from the literal meaning of the dialog.

✔ Reveal a character's mood

Speech patterns change, depending on whether a character is bored, exhilarated, wary, tired, alert, playful, tense, expectant, anxious, and so on. A character's moods can change several times during a scene, when the beat changes significantly.

✔ Reveal characters' relationships to each other

The way people speak with each other can reveal their relative places in the social hierarchy, their places within an organization, their relative power, and their emotional connection. Dialog can also reveal their attitudes towards each other. (Perhaps one character reacts to another with distrust, admiration, curiosity, resentment, jealousy, disdain, or pity.)

When characters' relationships to each other change during a play, their ways of speaking with each other change, too. Changes can occur several times in one conversation even if the relationship does not change significantly.

Consider the varying ways a person speaks to another when they are beginning a romance, when they are comfortably involved, when they are angry, when they are openly fighting, and after they have separated. If you have two lovers who go through those five stages without different ways of speaking to each other, you have some revision ahead of you.

> *Employment counselors point out that if you are interviewed by a team whose leader is not made known to you, you can often figure out who is the most important person. The unannounced leader is the one who most readily changes the subject, asks impromptu questions, or signals the end of the interview. The lowest ranking member of the interviewing team is unlikely to change a line of discussion begun by the boss, or make a funny remark. Ambitious staff members tend to mirror the body language and posture of the highest ranking person, and everyone laughs at even the weak jokes uttered by the leader.*

✔ Provide exposition

Exposition is information that the audience needs but that will not be enacted on stage. Exposition usually includes background information about characters and information about offstage events or events that happened before the opening of the play.

✔ Foreshadow events

Foreshadowing is planting ideas or suggestions that later occur as reality. As a simple example, the suicide of a character at the end of a play might be foreshadowed by allusions to suicide earlier in the play.

✔ Provide humor

People enjoy humor. Everyday conversation is marked by frequent intentional humor, and by considerable unintentional humor (at least to the perceptive observer). Even great tragedies have humor, and some have scenes that are entirely comic. Some playwrights believe that humor is necessary as *comic relief*, to make dramatic or tragic action tolerable.

✔ Contribute towards theme

Do not use dialog to reveal your theme by having a character state your ideas directly. In fact, your characters have no understanding that they are in a play, let alone what the play's theme is, so no character is likely to articulate the theme or speak for the playwright.

"If you are writing a propaganda play," one wise writer advised, "don't let your characters know."

✔ Help stage business

You might need to provide dialog of a certain length to divert attention from one part of the stage, or to provide an exiting actor time to change costumes. This should never be the sole purpose of any dialog.

Characters Have Unique Speaking Styles

Every person, including each of your characters, has unique speech mannerisms. Your characters should not sound alike. Distinct speech characteristics help illuminate character and provide a rich texture to your dialog. Remember how different the speech patterns of Hamlet, Polonius, and Ophelia are. Consider these possibilities:

✔ Verbal tics, characteristic phrases

A born again Christian might refer to something good as a "blessing." A young person, or someone wanting to seem young, might respond instead by just calling it "cool."

✔ Slang or standard English

Dialog can be a class indicator. Slang will eventually date your play, but you can worry about that later.

✔ Tendency to interrupt

People who like to control conversations, or are impatient, or are in charge tend to interrupt more frequently than do others. Research suggests that men tend to interrupt more than women. The more powerful person in a business relationship probably interrupts more than the less powerful.

✔ Non sequiturs

Some people's responses don't follow the previous remark, either because they have misunderstood, or they think in eccentric ways. Non sequiturs are a staple of comedy and of contemporary drama.

✔ Sweeping statements, clichés, platitudes

Some people tend to comment on events or close discussions with trite expressions like "the apple doesn't fall far from the tree." This does not suggest keen wit.

✔ Complete sentences or fragments

Educated people (especially if they are precise and orderly) tend to speak in complete sentences. Any character who is angry or desperate or excited is likely to use more fragments and phrases.

✔ Frequent references to herself or himself

Some people always turn conversations to themselves. If you tell them you just broke your leg, instead of asking how you are doing they will tell you about the time they almost broke their leg.

SPEECH MARKERS

Identify specific speech characteristics of five of your family or friends.

_____

_____

_____

_____

_____

Compare speech patterns of three neighbors, teachers, or colleagues.

_____

_____

_____

_____

_____

_____

Pauses and Silences

☑ ## Use pauses to create tension

One character's delay in answering another's serious question creates in the audience an urgency to hear the answer.

☑ ## Let brief silences create enigmas

What *are* they thinking?

☑ ## Put key words and ideas at the end of the sentence

The end of a sentence is more powerful than the beginning or middle, because the ensuing silence allows the last few words to echo in the audience's mind.

A principle of comedy is to put the punch at the very end of the sentence. This way, laughter won't drown out part of the delivery, and the humorous part won't be weakened. Watch a standup comic to see how this works.

Dramatic Irony

Dramatic irony is an especially wonderful aspect of dialog. It is the irony created when a character says one thing but the audience understands something very different. The classic example is Oedipus's public promise to avenge the murder of the king. The Greek audience knew that Oedipus was himself the killer, and that his promise meant his own destruction. Dramatic irony isn't always as dramatic as that. Think about how often, when you are listening to someone, you have reactions and perceptions far different from those intended.

✔ Examples of dramatic irony

"I always get bad waitresses."

Always? This says more about the self-pity and crabbiness of the speaker than about the waitresses.

"You just can't trust a chick."

"Chick" reveals a patronizing attitude towards women. The whole assertion implies a tendency towards sweeping generalities, and a sense of betrayal. The speaker has probably had a history of bad relationships with women.

"I love my husband, and stuff."

The slang "and stuff" at least weakens, and perhaps calls into question, the speaker's claim to love her husband.

"I ain't no uneducated jerk who don't know how to talk good."

This dialog not only tells us the *opposite* of what the speaker says, it also suggests that the speaker is defensive and hostile.

DRAMATIC IRONY

Write a one-page monolog in which a character from page 31 says one thing but reveals something very different

> (for example, a repressed person proclaiming how liberated he is). Don't be too obvious. Let us learn the truth towards the end of the monolog.

_____

_____

_____

_____

_____

_____

_____

_____

_____

_____

_____

_____

Subtext

Be sure that your dialog is rich in subtext! If your first draft seems flat and literal, with all the characters' feelings and intents openly spoken, revise to provide more subtext.

✔ Subtext is the meaning hidden between the lines

Harold Pinter tells us, and his plays wonderfully demonstrate, that words and actions are more often used to *conceal* our actual thoughts than to reveal them.

Imagine all of those conversations you have had in which you concealed important thoughts: conversations with parents, new romantic interests, police officers, job interviewers, children, supervisors, clients, professors, party hosts, and salespeople.

✔ Subtext gives the audience an active role

Your audience would rather discover character by reading between the lines than by having matters announced to them.

✔ Subtext is more interesting than explicit dialog

What are a parent and child arguing about when they argue about a messy room, or borrowing the car, or curfew? They are probably struggling over issues of independence, authority, freedom, and trust.

You can show characters' power relationships by having them decide a trivial matter, such as where to dine. Quarrels and struggles are more interesting when they are not shouting matches.

> *"If the scene is about what the scene is about, it's dead. Or if two characters say 'I love you' and mean it, the scene is over. A story must have subtext."*
>
> LINDA STUART

SUBTEXT

If you hear a little girl say, "You're the best daddy in the whole world," do you believe that . .

(a) He is the best daddy in the whole world.

(b) She loves her father.

Subtext is especially rich in dialog between two characters (or people) who are unwilling to be completely overt about their opinions, such as two people conducting a subtle and sarcastic argument without wanting others present to understand, or a man and a woman who have just met and find each other attractive.

Write down statements you have spoken to others today, or heard from others, that have subtext meanings.

_____

_____

_____

_____

_____

_____

_____

_____

Showing Emotions by Speech Disruptions

People often try to avoid expressing their true feelings. Insincerity alters their body language and creates speech disturbances, sometimes called "leakage" by speech pathologists. Leave the body-language decisions to the actors, but use speech disturbances in your dialog.

✔ Deceitful people show speech disruptions

Unless they are skilled liars and manipulators, people being deceitful show some or all of the following speech disturbances, according to researchers. They

- make fewer factual statements and more general ones
- speak less (probably out of worry about revealing too much)
- hesitate more, using more *uhs* and *ers*
- end sentences with a different syntactic pattern than they started with (for example, "I ate lunch early because . . .I was hungry, so I ate lunch early.")
- make slips of the tongue, using wrong words (including "Freudian slips")
- change word choice in midsentence (for example, "I met Sal . . . I met Ms. Smith.")

You already knew this! Your audience will understand what these speech disturbances mean, too, even if they've never had these patterns pointed out to them, because everyone learns to interpret verbal signals as they grow up.

In fact, even if you never read this page or heard about leakage elsewhere, you'd probably use some of these devices, because at a subconscious level you know how being deceitful or cautious can create specific speech disturbances.

✔ People who are uncertain or anxious might show similar leakage

Exposition

✔ Present exposition subtly and naturally

Don't let your audience realize that they are getting a dose of exposition. Exposition should be carefully concealed within dialog that has other purposes, and not all spewed out at once.

✘ Don't rush exposition

It is *not* necessary that the audience immediately know all of the significant events that happened before the curtain.

Contemporary playwrights tend to introduce exposition much later than did their predecessors.

✘ Don't wait too late

Providing certain critical exposition too late can irritate the audience. Playwrights writing mysteries are careful to plant critical background facts relatively early, so that those facts do not appear to be desperate, last-minute contrivances by the author to explain action, and so that the facts are not fresh in the audience's mind at the climax of the play.

✔ Provide important information

The famous "rule of three" holds that the playwright must have a fact mentioned three times to insure that no one in the audience misses it. Don't take the *three* too literally. Once might even be enough.

THEME

✔ Theme is a central idea, insight, or observation

Every literary work has a theme, whether the author ever thinks about it or not. Your play might have a major theme, and one or more minor themes as well, depending upon whom you ask. In some of the best plays, major themes and minor themes are complementary, just like plot and subplot.

✔ Theme should evolve naturally out of your characters and plot

Although theme is an essential part of your play, you are better off not thinking about it while you are writing. Your play *will* have a theme, but you do not need to know what it is while you are writing!

Your best play will probably come out of exploring what happens to people in certain interesting circumstances. You are more likely to write a good story thinking *I'll write about a teenager deciding what to do about her alcoholic sister* than if you start out to write a polemical piece to convert readers to your position on alcoholism or sisterhood. If you write your play freely, without a thematic purpose, you might even discover ideas and feelings that you had not known before.

> *"If you want to send a message, use Western Union."*
> D. W. GRIFFITH
>
> *"Theme is the result, look for it last."*
> DAVID BALL

✔ A theme is not a "moral" or bumper sticker philosophy

Aesop's fables end with simple morals, such as "the race is not always won by the swift," but your play is not a fable.

Few good plays have themes comparable to bumper stickers that express an aphoristic philosophy *(Life sucks and then you die)*, express a value *(A man of quality is not threatened by a woman of equality)*, or issue a command *(Fight AIDS, not people with AIDS)*.

Television shows are simplistic enough to have facile, easily stated themes, such as "crime does not pay" or "people with fatal diseases should not give up hope." But any play whose theme can be neatly summed up on a bumper sticker is not likely to be very interesting.

> *"Doubtless an author's politics must be one element, and even an important one, in the germination of his art, but if it is art he has created, it must by definition bend itself to his observation, rather than to his opinions or even his hopes."*
>
> ARTHUR MILLER

✔ A theme need not be a position on an issue

It is quite enough to *explore* a condition or predicament, or to *show what it is like* to be in a particular circumstance.

> *"The purpose of creative expression is not to answer questions but to ask them."*
>
> RICHARD WALTER

✔ Your story's theme can be unconventional or controversial

All mass-market art, especially television, depends on pleasing vast numbers of people, and so it offers simple themes that comfort and reassure the majority of the audience. Television networks and sponsors demand it. Imagine a crime series in which crime *does* pay, one in which law enforcement agents are incompetent patsies, while the drug dealers who laugh at them are intelligent, admirable, and heroic. You might imagine it, but you'll never see it.

And do not expect mass-market art to suggest that socialism is better than capitalism, that love does not last, or that corrupt senators are really good people. Screenwriters are restricted to accepted ideas and values.

Mass art tells people what they want to hear. People want to believe that love can last, the rebel can defeat corrupt and powerful forces, all of our soldiers are heroes, crime does not pay, and our culture is better than other cultures.

But you might not believe all of this yourself. Much of the world's best literature explores dark ideas that run counter to the accepted values of the writers' own times and cultures.

As a playwright, you are free to explore any theme you want. This is the good news.

"Your play should either entertain, question, or challenge, and at best, do all three."

JANET NEIPRIS

✔ Themes can affect your play's chances of being produced. So what?

The bad news is that the values inherent in your play, like its language, might prevent you from finding a theater to produce it. But this restriction is probably less troublesome to you than to any of the great playwrights of the past. Every culture has directly or indirectly restricted what playwrights could do. In every era, society and government have exerted pressure on artists to confirm to accepted social beliefs.

In the United States today, it is not the government but the marketplace (or theaters' beliefs about their marketplace) that is likely to exert pressure. Those beliefs do change over time. Let's not dismiss this with a sneer as political correctness. Regardless of political ideology, *every* group has certain core values it does not want to help attack.

Most professional theaters rely on corporate support and subscription ticket sales to the middle class, so they are sensitive to the tastes and interests of their patrons. College theater groups are also reluctant to offend the campus community, trustees, and alumni.

Your theme might complicate your efforts to get your play produced, but you cannot let that inhibit your writing. Worry about production *after* the play is written. Let the play become what it wants to be. Once it is finished, you can transform yourself from playwright to agent.

"Really, you don't know what the plays are about until you have written them. They tell you what they're about."

CHRISTOPHER HAMPTON

"I'm not suggesting that the theater should be deliberately provocative, but if it's not provoking someone, then it's probably not doing its job, which is to rearrange consciousness."

ROBERT BRUSTEIN

WRITING YOUR
FIRST PLAY

SELECT AND EVALUATE YOUR IDEA

Select one of the situations you created on page 19, or an idea you have had since. Test it against the following questions. If it fails, try a different idea.

Is it theatrical or just dramatic?

Many events are *dramatic*, but you would not want to see a play about them because they are not *theatrical*: a skier breaking a leg, a dog in pain, a snake in your bathtub.

A story is *theatrical* if it is appropriate for stage representation. A train wreck is more dramatic than a lovers' quarrel, but a quarrel is more theatrical than a train wreck.

Does it offer emotion, spectacle, and ideas?

Most effective plays offer at least some of all three.

Emotion is central to effective theater, unless you are writing a special-effects Broadway extravaganza, or believe that your political play's lesson would be weakened if your audience felt rather than thought.

Spectacle is the visual element of your play, a combination of the set *(mise-en-scène)* and stage movement. Most contemporary Broadway plays (for example, *Cats*) seem to emphasize this, but your play presumably will not. Pure spectacle is the stuff of drill teams and jugglers.

If your story idea is to make good theater, there must be *some* visual interest, some stage movement, even if the stage is bare of props and scenery.

Ideas can lift a play beyond transitory pleasures (like those of a television chase scene) by providing insight into the human condition. Your play does *not* have to have an obvious, easily paraphrased idea, and probably should not. A play rich in ideas lets its audience encounter, discover, realize, confront, and understand. Don't let your ideas overwhelm your play.

Can you avoid sentimentality and melodrama?

Sentiment is good, but *sentimentality* is too much sentiment for the occasion. Anyone can evoke cheap sentimentality, which has no place in your play.

Sentimental works insist on their own sincerity, but are insincere.

Melodrama is sensationalism, sentimentality, and exaggerated emotions. Early films with villainous landlords tying helpless orphans to railroad tracks exploited melodrama.

Avoid trying to write a play whose premise will make it difficult for you to avoid sentimentality and melodrama.

> *"All bad art is sincere."*
> OSCAR WILDE

Is it interesting to you?

Can you write to discover rather than to tell what you already know?

One of the great pleasures of writing, helping to compensate for its difficulty, is the joy of discovery. Writers discover what they have to say by writing, not before writing. For this reason you will probably benefit most from writing about an important matter that you haven't quite figured out yet.

If instead you write to convince others of something you firmly believe, you will probably bore yourself before having the opportunity to bore an audience.

Audiences enjoy good theater in part because it leads them to discover what they never really knew, or because it illuminates what they vaguely sensed, even if what they discover is dark and troubling. Playwrights should enjoy and benefit from this discovery just as their audiences do.

DECIDE HOW TO WRITE YOUR FIRST DRAFT

✔ You can just start writing

Select a situation and start writing. Let your characters determine their fates and the development of the plot.

If you write their dialog honestly, from within the characters rather than from a godlike knowledge of how matters will turn out, they might say and do wonderful things you could not have imagined in any other way.

Using this method, you might, on the other hand, waste many hours writing dialog going nowhere in scenes that you have to discard, without in the process discovering a useful story or developing interesting characters.

This is probably a good method if you prefer the excitement of discovery to the comfort of foreknowledge, if you have an interesting situation but are perplexed about how it might evolve, and if you will not be discouraged if your first few efforts do not become plays. **Go to page 85**.

✔ You can plan the plot and scene sequence ahead of time

Turn your situation into story, and your story into plot, using the prompts in the next few pages.

Knowing exactly what you need to accomplish in each scene will keep you focused, and probably allow you to create a first draft needing fewer major revisions.

This method makes it more difficult for you to discover new possibilities, lessens the excitement of creative risk taking, and might lull you into creating two-dimensional characters who seem trapped by their fates rather than who create their own.

This is probably a good method if you anticipate difficulties with structure, know how you want the dramatic question to be resolved, dread writing whole scenes that will have to be discarded, and are more comfortable with clear guidelines than with absolute freedom.

If You Decide to Plan Carefully

☑ **Select a situation that interests you from page 19**

☑ **Select the theatrical, not the dramatic**

Some real-life events are theatrical, but only in the sense that they involve ritual, emotion, and spectacle: a presidential inauguration, a wedding, a boxing match.

The playwright needs to find a story that is theatrical, that involves emotions, ritual, and conflict: a story that can be created on stage (providing the spectacle).

> *"Busy yourself with something more interesting and less exciting."*
>
> KONSTANTIN STANISLAVSKY

☑ **Choose an emotional, rather than physical, conflict**

✔ Consider writing about an analog to your story

Most play's stories are variations of a few fundamental human experiences and human issues.

You can explore a fundamental issue without trying to replicate the specifics. If a romantic triangle reminds you of an election campaign, try writing about a romantic triangle by writing a play about an election campaign.

✔ Select a working title

✔ Turn your story into plot

TURNING STORY INTO PLOT

List the major events of your story

_____

_____

_____

_____

_____

_____

_____

_____

_____

_____

_____

_____

_____

_____

Select your protagonist

In theory, any character in a story could be the protagonist. Pick the one that interests you the most, the one with the most interesting character, objective, and obstacles.

_____

Identify the dramatic question

You might have several to choose from. Some potential dramatic questions might be used as a subplot, or left unanswered at the end of the play.

_____

_____

_____

Identify the inciting incident

The inciting incident triggers those events that throw off the delicate balance of your characters' lives. It can occur before or in the play's opening scene.

_____

_____

_____

_____

_____

Select the scene that will be your crisis

Is there an obligatory scene in which the protagonist confronts the antagonist or must make the central decision or perform the decisive act? Your crisis scene will be the point of highest tension, shortly after which the play will end.

_____

_____

_____

_____

_____

_____

_____

_____

_____

_____

_____

_____

_____

Evaluate each earlier event (p. 80) for inclusion or omission

1. How does the event advance the plot or reveal character?

2. Can the event's important elements be provided in exposition rather than shown directly?

3. Is the event likely to be an effective scene, having conflict and physical action, and a little plot of its own?

4. Does it bring together two characters who otherwise would not appear on stage together?

5. Does it require a new set?

List the scenes you have tentatively decided to include

_____

_____

_____

_____

_____

_____

_____

_____

How many sets are required?

Consider re-selecting scenes, or changing your plans for them, so that all of the scenes involve the same set.

Evaluate your tentative structure for the elements of plot

Is there rising action? Does the crisis occur right before the end of the play? Are there smaller crises and climaxes before the major one?

_____

Write your final list of scenes

Well, "final" in the planning stage. You might change your mind as you write the play.

_____

_____

_____

_____

_____

_____

_____

If You Decide to Write Freely

✔️ **Select an interesting situation, character, or image**

✔️ **Select a working title**

> *"For myself, it has never been possible to generate the energy to write and complete a play if I know in advance everything it signifies and all that it will contain. The very impulse to write, I think, springs from an inner chaos crying for order, for meaning, and that meaning must be discovered in the process of writing . . ."*
>
> ARTHUR MILLER

> *"When I start a play, beyond an entirely general pattern, I have little or no idea what will become of my characters individually at the end. I generally follow their progress with a more or less benign interest and hope that the staging and construction will be taken care of by some divine subconscious automatic pilot."*
>
> ALAN AYCKBOURN

Select a Working Title

Your title is *extraordinarily* important. Even if you hate to create titles, you must work on this until you have the very best title possible.

✔️ **Your title can improve your chance to be produced**

Intrigue the literary manager who picks up your script from the mail so much that he or she *wants* the play to be good.

✔️ **Your title can attract greater audiences**

Until your name is enough to attract audiences, you must rely on titles to intrigue people enough to buy tickets.

✔ Your title can suggest your subject, genre, or tone

Does your title promise a comedy? Romance? Mystery? What might a theatergoer expect from a play entitled *Betrayal*, or *Blithe Spirit*, or *Danton's Death*, or *Desire Under the Elms*? Consider the expectations aroused by certain words, like "betrayal" and "blithe" and "desire."

✔ Your title can influence the audience's understanding

Your title can emphasize a symbol or suggest a theme.

✔ Puzzles, paradoxes, and surprises create interest

Who's Afraid of Virginia Woolf? curiously conflates a nursery rhyme and modern author, and no one yet knows quite what the title means. *The School for Scandal* surprises us because there is no such school.

SIX TRADITIONAL SOURCES FOR TITLES

✔ The central story, idea, or focus

Death of a Salesman
Mrs. Warren's Profession
A Delicate Balance

✔ A metaphor for the central story

The Taming of the Shrew
A Doll's House
Long Day's Journey into Night

✔ Characters

King Lear
The Misanthrope
Three Sisters

A place name

> *Talley's Folly*
> *Glengarry Glen Ross*
> *Three Hotels*

 A symbol in the play

> *The Cherry Orchard*
> *The Glass Menagerie*
> *A Streetcar Named Desire*

 An intriguing phrase from the dialog

> *Suddenly, Last Summer*
> *Who's Afraid of Virginia Woolf?*
> *'night, Mother*

A WORKING TITLE

Write down one possible title from each source. Then select one as your working title. If you don't like it, you will be motivated to think of a better title later.

The central story, idea, or focus
Possible title: _____

Metaphor for the central story
Possible title: _____

Character or characters
Possible title: _____

Place name
Possible title: _____

Symbol in the play
Possible title: _____

Intriguing phrase you plan to use in the dialog
Possible title: _____

WRITE YOUR FIRST DRAFT

✔ Use the proper format

Appendix A shows how your script might look. There are other formats, but they differ only slightly.

✔ Be free

Whether or not you have planned your play in detail, be open to inspiration, discovery, spontaneity, and risk. If your characters want to say or do something new, let them. Try to write from within the character, not like a manipulative god or puppet-master.

✔ Finish your first draft before doing any revising

Don't lose your momentum. If you hit a rough spot while creating, you'll be tempted to go back over what you have already written. Be strong. Go forward.

> *"Not one damned word has ever written itself."*
>
> ARTHUR PLOTNIK

> *"You can rewrite a play for the rest of your life, but for that first draft, you put the pedal to the metal. I don't write plays in 48 hours any more, but I write in two or three weeks. I need that momentum."*
>
> PAULA VOGEL

Troubleshooting

✔ Don't know how to finish?

If you wrote your draft without planning it first, go through the workpoints on pages 80–84. Pay special attention to the dramatic question and the climax.

Ask yourself the classic stumped writer's question, "What if?" That is, imagine a new character, a new complication, a new obstacle. What different character flaw might nicely complicate your protagonist's pursuit of the objective?

✔ Finished, but the play's too brief?

If your play seems complete, and is likely to run 20 to 60 minutes, you might just have a one-act play, even if you had expected a full length play of at least 90 minutes.

Consider adding one or more scenes that are inherent in the story but not shown on stage.

Do your characters rush to get to the point? Consider slowing conversations to exploit the potentials of subtext and tension.

Does your action rush from the opening to the crisis without adequate complications? Discover appropriate complications.

✔ Finished, but the play's too long?

No problem. Read the section on revision.

Writer's Block

If one day you feel that you just cannot coax words out at all, welcome to writer's block. Don't expect sympathy from other writers or understanding from nonwriters. Just find a cure fast.

✔ Schedule time to write

Do nothing except *write*, not even *related* activities. Do not read about writing, sharpen your pencil, look up theaters, or tinker with what you have already.

✔ Make a contract to reward writing and punish sloth

Establish rewards and punishments for specific goals. Determine your goal for the day (perhaps ten pages of script), and list the rewards you will give yourself for success. Include the special pleasures of your day, enough to motivate you to accomplish your goal.

You can also decide to do onerous tasks if you fail to meet your day's objective.

Some writers set aside a certain amount of money. If they meet their goals, they get to spend the money on clothes or wine or dining out. If they fail to meet their goals, they give the money to someone else. If you use this system, *tell* that someone else.

Set a reasonably demanding goal. These contracts should not intimidate you into trying for too little; they should motivate you to do a full day's work.

✔ Set a specific goal (pages or scenes, not time)

Set your goal in pages or tasks. If you say, "I'll write until noon," it is too easy to do nothing until noon. Decide instead, "I'll write until I finish a draft of this scene."

✔ Work on a different script

You probably have more than one play in mind anyway. If you're stymied on one, loosen up by working on another. Maybe you'll go back once you are warmed up, but even if you do not, you will be succeeding at something rather than being frustrated.

Like Sam Shepard, many playwrights admit to having dozens of unfinished play beginnings in their closets. Unless *all* of your plays are unfinished, this is not a problem. Unless you have a compelling reason to stay with one play, you'll probably find that writer's block is rather easily overcome by temporarily working on something else.

✔ Avoid avoidance techniques

You know what your favorite avoidance techniques are. Make a list of your favorite time wasters.

Imagine yourself at a cocktail party telling someone "I say that I want to write a play but instead I watch *Jeopardy*."

If you are unwilling to give up some of your time wasters, make them part of your rewards contract with yourself. If you do not have the first act done by Friday, you will not watch television over the weekend.

> *"Don't get it right, get it written."*
> JAMES THURBER

EVALUATE YOUR DRAFT

✔ Put it aside for a while

Writing is very difficult to assess soon after it has been written.

✔ Write your general impression in your journal

Write this, rather than just think about it, so that your thoughts are clear.

✔ Use the checklist to examine specifics

See page 93.

✔ Read your play backwards

Start at the last line, and make sure that every line of dialog derives naturally from what comes before it. If this system seems odd or not worth your trouble, read David Ball's *Backwards and Forwards*, which should convince you.

☑ Reread earlier sections of this book

Some of the principles and practices will make more sense to you after you have written a first draft than they did before.

☑ Ask others' opinions

Listen to their responses, without defending yourself or explaining your intentions. Encourage their frankness. (Say "That's interesting," and don't scowl.) Take notes, or ask them to give you an informal written response.

After someone has finished volunteering her or his opinions, ask specific questions about areas that trouble you. ("Is that character too domineering?")

Evaluation Checklist

Do this evaluation thoughtfully. Start with these major questions, checking off the box next to any problem area. When you have finished the evaluation and are ready to revise, reread the appropriate section of the book.

You might also find this evaluation useful in critiquing a play you have just seen.

The story

☐ Is the situation interesting rather than trite?
☐ Does the situation involve universal human experiences?
☐ Is the interest rooted in emotions rather than physical action?
☐ Does the play go past the shallow, into the secret lives of the characters?

The dramatic question

☐ Is it made clear early in the play?
☐ Is it important enough to sustain audience interest?

☐ Is the outcome in doubt, rather than predictable?
☐ Is the dramatic question resolved at the climax?

All characters (evaluate them one at a time)

☐ Are all drawn fairly?
☐ Does each act, react, and speak individually?
☐ Are changes in mood, belief, or objective plausible?

Major characters

☐ Is each interesting and unique, not a stereotype?
☐ Does each have an important objective?

The protagonist

☐ Does the protagonist's objective drive the play?
☐ Is the protagonist's objective emotionally important?
☐ Does the protagonist have interesting (and relevant) flaws and weaknesses?
☐ Does the protagonist largely determine the outcome?

The antagonist

☐ Is she or he fairly drawn, with some good qualities?

Plot

☐ Are there enough complications?
☐ Are the complications relevant and interesting?
☐ Is there rising action towards the climax?
☐ Are there no long periods without forward progress?
☐ Is the pace fast enough to maintain interest?
☐ Is the pace restrained enough to generate suspense?

If there is a subplot

☐ Is it relevant to the main plot?

Acts

☐ Does the first act end with a new device heightening suspense?
☐ Are the first act's final lines effective?
☐ Does the division into acts fall naturally?
☐ Is the last act shorter than the first?

Scenes

☐ Is each scene worth including (not better replaced by minor exposition)?
☐ Is the obligatory scene included?
☐ Does each scene have a late point of attack?
☐ Are the most important scenes given more time than minor scenes?
☐ Does each scene have its own rising action and climax?
☐ Does each character have an objective at the beginning of each scene?

Play length and playing time

☐ Is the length appropriate for a one-act (15–60 minutes) or full length (90+ minutes) play?

The beginning and the end

☐ Does the opening immediately engage audience interest?
☐ Do you introduce conflict very early?
☐ Is the denouement brief enough to maintain interest?
☐ Is the end free of characters announcing the theme for you?

Dialog

☐ Does every line perform more than one function?
☐ Is the script rich with subtext?
☐ Does the play use dramatic irony for character revelation?
☐ Does each character have a distinct voice?

☐ Is the language pleasing to the ear?
☐ Is there any unnecessary repetition?

Theme

☐ Does the theme arise naturally from the action?

Title

☐ Is the working title appropriate and intriguing? Absolutely irreplaceable?

REVISION GOALS

Identify your major revision goals

_____

_____

_____

_____

_____

_____

_____

_____

_____

_____

_____

_____

_____

_____

_____

REVISE YOUR PLAY

✔ Plays aren't written, they're rewritten

This might be the first rule of playwriting. Revision isn't a brief chore to be done quickly, but an ongoing process. Every time you hear your play given a reading or performed, you will discover ways to improve it.

✔ Make large changes first

Solve the major problems first. In doing that, you might discard entire scenes or significantly change characters. Don't waste time tinkering with lines that might be replaced.

✔ Rewrite weak scenes before tinkering with them

If you now have a better understanding of the function of a weak scene, try rewriting it from scratch. The novelist John Braine once said that he wrote the first draft of a novel to discover how it really should be written, and then threw out that first draft.

Your second version might be much better. Even if it is not, your new version might contain many lines of fine dialog that you would not have written had you focused too narrowly on revising your first draft.

"Love the art in yourself, not yourself in the art."
KONSTANTIN STANISLAVSKY

"I went to a Picasso exhibit, and there were some preliminary sketches that he made for one of his famous paintings. They started with a complete drawing of a woman, and each of the succeeding 200 drawings subtracted elements of this person until she is finally represented by just a few essential lines."
JEREMY WHELAN

DEVELOP YOUR PLAY

The play development stage of playwriting begins when you get other people involved with your efforts to improve your script. Play development usually starts with an informal reading and can later involve staged readings and workshop productions.

Your script gets only one chance with each theater, so don't submit a script that you know needs work. Once a theater group accepts your script, *don't* ask them to hold off because you are in the middle of rewriting.

☑ Make sure your play is as good as it can be before development

If you know you still have some specific tinkering to do, do it first.

☑ Prepare your script and ancillary materials professionally

Using a standard format will help actors at your readings and will eventually help convince the literary manager that your play wasn't written by an amateur. See Appendix A for a good format.

The ancillary materials (including a synopsis, cover letter, and playwright biography) do not have to be prepared until you submit your script to a contest or theater.

☑ Find or create local reading opportunities

Before you send your script to a theater, have actors do a reading for you. You will learn from each reading, make some contacts, and perhaps get your script talked about. Actors' suggestions after a reading can be very valuable. If your readings have audiences in addition to the actors involved, you can learn even more (such as which lines draw laughs). Without prompting, some people will tell you which lines or moments were especially powerful.

✔ Research theater groups

After one or more informal readings, and whatever rewritings those readings prompted you to do, look for a theater group interested in doing a more formal reading, a workshop production or, if you are lucky, a regular production.

Read *The Playwright's Companion* and *Dramatists Sourcebook* for theater groups whose interests and capabilities fit your play. Ask out-of-town friends to send reviews of local plays so that you can learn more about what other theater groups do. Reviews can also provide you with a fact or two to mention in your query letter and a chance to tell the theater why you think they might like your script.

An increasing number of theaters these days host play readings as fund-raisers (they charge admission, but do not pay the readers or playwright) or as showcases in which actors and playwrights showcase their talents for any producers or directors in the audience.

✔ Find contests

The same books list contests, some of which involve production for winning plays. Winning a contest can help sell your script to a theater group.

Unfortunately, contest entries involve fees – which is why most of the contests exist in the first place. Some theaters allegedly use the contest structure as a way of getting reading fees from playwrights, rather than simply reading unsolicited manuscripts for free in their search for plays to produce.

Prepare Your Script and Ancillary Materials

✔ Format your script

See Appendix A.

✔ Write a synopsis

The synopsis gives a theater's literary manager a quick idea of whether or not your play fits their interests and capabilities. The theater wants to know both the overall story of the play and such nuts-and-bolts issues as cast size. See Appendix B.

✔ Write a query letter

Some theaters ask for a query letter, not the script. The query letter should be written as carefully as any other sales letter: if your query letter interests the theater, they will invite you to send the script itself.

While you will send essentially the same query letter to every theater, try to personalize it when possible.

✔ Write a cover letter

Always include a cover letter when you send your script, along with whatever other materials are requested (usually a synopsis, script history, and playwright biography).

The cover letter should give the theater a sense of who you are, and any experience that is relevant to your play.

✔ Prepare a script history

Some theaters ask for a *script history*, which can be mentioned in your query or cover letter, or prepared as a separate document if the script has had many readings and productions.

Obviously, a play with several productions by major regional theaters will gain attention.

If your play has never been produced, at least you can offer a theater the world premier. Even the most frequently produced plays in America were once in search of their first production.

Production Options

✔ Host a cold reading

Friends (especially actor friends) can gather in your living room to read the script without rehearsal, much as a theater group would do a read-through when it first begins rehearsal. You'll learn about your play from hearing them read and from their questions and suggestions.

✔ Arrange a public reading

Provide an informal reading at a local community center, church, coffee shop, or college, followed by a discussion. The readers should meet for one or two rehearsals, which will also be learning occasions for you. Now you have a bit of script history.

✔ Seek a workshop production

Offer your play to college theater programs and to acting studios. Actors in training, led by competent teachers, can help you as you fine-tune your work.

✔ Find a theater

A little research and common sense will help you identify those theaters most likely to want your script. This can be a lengthy process. Until directories are on line, start with *The Playwright's Companion* and *Dramatists Sourcebook.*

✔ Produce your own play

If you have spare money, extra time, and some background in theater, you can become your own producer.

HOST A COLD READING

✔ Ask people to read specific roles

Get actors to do this, if you know some actors. If not, ask people you know who have some theater experience, if only as audiences. If that fails, enlist anyone.

✔ Ask other people to be an audience

The more, the better, especially if your play is a comedy.

✔ Give each reader a copy of your play ahead of time

In each actor's copy, highlight his or her character's name to minimize the disruptions caused when a reader fails to note a cue. Ask each to read the play a few times beforehand to get a sense of the character. If your readers have no acting training, tell each what her or his character is like, and what her or his relationship is to the other characters.

✔ Solicit opinions and suggestions afterwards

Have another person act as emcee to introduce the reading, read any essential stage directions, and lead the post-reading discussion. The emcee will explain that the playwright will benefit from hearing honest opinions, that in some ways an audience is a better judge of a play than is the playwright.

You should not identify yourself, so as not to stifle discussion; but if the audience knows you, smile and write down everyone's remarks, whether you like them or not. Don't get into the discussion yourself, explain the play, or defend certain choices you made. Don't commit to making any specific changes, but let people know how much you appreciate their help. If you have any specific question, have the emcee save it for last, after the audience and readers have finished their spontaneous remarks.

The praise is nice, but you will learn more from the suggestions for improvement, even if you reject them all. Gently avoid questions about your theme. Let *them* tell *you*.

ARRANGE A PUBLIC READING

✔ Offer to perform a reading and play discussion for a local group

Try a community theater group, literary club, or retirement community. Arrange for a performance space at a local college, bookstore, or coffeehouse.

✔ Arrange for readers

Some might come from the group for which you are performing.

✔ Rehearse

The rehearsals are an excellent opportunity to learn whether your dialog is speakable, and to get the readers' suggestions.

✔ Promote the reading with flyers and newspaper notices

You want the largest audience possible to get as many responses as possible. Maybe somebody from a theater group will attend and like your play.

✔ Arrange for a discussion leader

Not you. Your job is to sit in the back and take notes about how people respond, and what they suggest. Provide the discussion leader with one or two broad questions for the audience in case they are slow starters.

FIND A THEATER

Finding a theater to produce your work is the last event in a long process of play development. Be sure that your script is truly ready before sending it to theaters.

Keep in mind that theaters cannot produce every good work that arrives in the mail. In addition to looking for fine writing and compelling characters, literary managers have to consider several other matters, such as what their audiences want or the name recognition of the playwright. Some theaters schedule only one new play each season, and some do not perform new plays at all.

✔ Scout local theaters

Get to know the people there. Volunteer to distribute programs, help build sets, or do other tasks. You will learn valuable theater skills and do some networking that might eventuate in a production or introduce you to actors who will do readings for you.

✔ Attend theaters and read reviews when traveling

This is the best way to learn about theater groups, what they like to produce, and how good they are.

✔ Research theaters you cannot visit

Buy and carefully read *The Playwright's Companion* and *Dramatists Sourcebook*, which have entries for hundreds of theaters that are willing to consider scripts. Read *American Theater* and the *Dramatists Guild Quarterly*.

✔ Organize your mailings

Because getting a play produced is a long process, you should create an efficient system to track your play submissions. Appendix C will do nicely.

List in order the theater groups you plan to offer the script to, so that when one copy is returned to you rejected, you can send a fresh copy out immediately. If you have not already decided where to send your script next, you might put off locating the next theater and lose valuable time.

Have one clean copy ready to send when you get a rejection, but don't prepare too many spare copies, because you are likely to make minor changes at any time.

WHAT NEXT?

☑ **Begin your second play while promoting the first**

It might take several years to get your first play produced. Maybe forever. In the meantime, write your second.

☑ **Try new techniques**

Once you understand fundamental theater principles, look for ways to use them more fully and for ways to transcend them.

"Artists who do not go forward go backward."
KONSTANTIN STANISLAVSKY

SCRIPT FORMAT

PRELUDES, IMPROVISATIONS, INVENTIONS

a play in two acts

by Stephen Sossaman

Stephen Sossaman
Westfield State College
Westfield MA 01086-1630
(W) 413-572-5335
(H) 555-1212
ssossaman@wisdom.wsc.mass.edu

ACT I, SCENE 1

At curtain, Harry pours cognac into a whiskey glass and brings it over to the sofa; John in the armchair, is holding another. The two men act rather formal with each other. Harry is careful, rather wary; John is ingratiating, but not fully engaged in the conversation. John absentmindedly worries a rolled-up newspaper.

HARRY

Hope you don't mind, I'm switching to the cognac.

(HARRY pours generously into a whiskey glass and heads to the stage-left end of the sofa.)

JOHN

Oh, fine, please, go ahead. Anything at all.

HARRY

In fact, I don't think I've ever had Delamain cognac.

(JOHN, startled, rises quickly, goes to the liquor cabinet, examines the bottle, and tucks it away behind another bottle.)

JOHN

Delamain! That superb bottle is usually reserved for special occasions.

HARRY

Not bad (takes a full gulp).

JOHN

I should say not. That cognac is forty-five years old.

HARRY

Very tasty.

(JOHN goes back to his chair.)

                        JOHN

"Tasty." Yes. It is the finest cognac available.

                        HARRY

I wouldn't know. I don't get to travel much.

                        JOHN

(seeing Harry's glass) It's even better drunk <u>slowly</u>
in a brandy snifter.

                        HARRY

That hardly seems possible.

                        JOHN

A snifter lets the bouquet gather more strenuously and
<u>slowly</u>.

                        HARRY

(disinterested) Yeah? (taking a big gulp) I never was
much into sniffing bouquets.

                        JOHN

Enjoying the bouquet allows the experience to last
longer.

                        HARRY

(rising) What the hell. There's always more where that
came from.

          (HARRY walks back to the liquor cabinet and
          finds the Delamain)

SAMPLE SYNOPSIS

PRELUDES, IMPROVISATIONS, INVENTIONS

Synopsis

This naturalistic drama/comedy explores the duplicitous relationships among four people, revealed primarily through the seesaw verbal struggle between two men. Each battles to save his marriage, not so much from his adversary as from himself.

A stranger tells John, a self-absorbed painter in career decline, that he has been having an affair with John's wife, Anne.

The next day Anne and Harry (a board member at the symphony where Anne volunteers) come to Anne's home. They unexpectedly find John home early. Anne has no idea that Harry is the man who visited John the previous day, and so introduces the two men as if all were well. Neither man tells Anne that Harry was the stranger.

Harry reveals to John that he is not in fact Anne's lover, and explains his motive: payback for John's having had a real affair with Harry's wife, Margaret. Now the two men engage in a more complex and important struggle over Anne to preserve their egos and their marriages and to emerge triumphant over the other. Everything they say has a meaning hidden to Anne.

Culminating a tense series of parries and bluffs, Harry coerces John into an act that will finally clarify these ambiguous relationships. In the last scene, several months later, Margaret unexpectedly visits Anne. As they, too, both seek and dissemble, we discover the truth.

RECORD OF SUBMISSIONS

Play title:

Theater:

Date sent:

Acknowledgement postcard received:

Decision notification expected by:

Notes:

ADDRESSES AND WEB SITES

Inclusion here does not mean that these pages are endorsed. Use your own judgment.

Feedback Theatrebooks
305 Madison Avenue, Suite 1146
New York NY 10165
http://www.hypernet.com/prospero.html
> Publishers of *The Playwright's Companion,* an annual listing of theaters, contests, and other script opportunities.

Poets & Writers
http://www.pw.org
> This site includes a "Speakeasy" to meet other writers. The playwriting threads are quite rare compared to fiction and poetry.

The Dramatists Guild
1501 Broadway, Suite 701
New York NY 10036
http://www.dramaguild.com
> An organization of playwrights, and publisher of a directory of theaters and contests.

Theatre Communications Group
http://www.tcg.org
> Publishers of *Dramatists Sourcebook*

The Playwriting Seminars
http://www.vcu.edu/artweb/playwriting/seminar.html

Playwrights on the Web
http://www.stageplays.com/writers.htm

Theater Links
http://www.poewar.com/links/scriptwriting.htm
http://www.dramex.org/theatrelinks.html
http://www.lsw.org.uk/links.htm
http://www.rlc.dcccd.edu/human/thehot.htm

AN EXAMPLE: IBSEN'S *A DOLL'S HOUSE*

Playwrights can learn a great deal by deconstructing some effective plays. Look for the principles identified in this book.

The story underlying Henrik Ibsen's *A Doll's House*

Here is the series of events that comprise the *story* of the play, in approximately chronological order. The playwright had to decide which events to stage in scenes, and which to reveal through exposition. If this entire story were told, we'd have an intolerably long and unfocused play.

1. In his youth, Torvald Helmer is friendly with Nils Krogstad.

2. Torvald and Nils end their friendship.

3. In her youth, Nora is friendly with Kristine.

4. Kristine and Nils become romantically involved.

5. Needing financial security, Kristine leaves Nils to marry a Mr. Linde out of town.

6. Nora's father is involved in a financial scandal.

7. Nora marries the older Torvald.

8. Nils gets a job at the bank.

9. Torvald becomes very ill, and must go to a warmer climate to survive.

10. Nora's father dies.

11. Nora forges her father's signature to borrow money from Nils to finance a trip to Italy.

12. Nora and Torvald spend a year in Italy, where he recovers his health.

13. Nora and Torvald, back home, have three children.

14. Nora skims household funds and secretly earns money by sewing and knitting.

15. Nora secretly makes periodic loan repayments to Nils.

16. Dr. Rank (Nora and Torvald's closest friend) secretly falls in love with Nora.

17. Kristine's husband dies, and she struggles financially.

18. Nils is caught in a forgery, suffering disgrace.

19. Nils develops a reputation as a blackmailer.

20. Dr. Rank contracts a life-threatening illness.

21. Torvald is offered a fine job as the bank's manager, starting in a few months.

22. Kristine, back in town, asks Nora to have Torvald arrange a job for her at the bank.

23. Torvald agrees to find a clerical bank job for Kristine.

24. Nils asks Nora to prevent Torvald from firing him when he becomes manager.

25. Nora intercedes for Nils, but fails: his job is the one Kristine is to get.

26. Dr. Rank tells Nora that he awaits one more test to confirm that he is dying.

27. Dr. Rank tells Nora that he adores her.

28. Nils tells Nora he will not surrender her forgery, even when the loan is fully paid.

29. Nils writes a letter to Torvald, revealing the secret and demanding not to be fired.

30. Nils drops the letter in Torvald's locked mailbox.

31. Nils agrees to Kristine's suggestion that they marry and leave town.

32. Dr. Rank reveals to Nora that he is, indeed, dying, and will die alone.

33. Torvald reads Nils' letter, and angrily confronts Nora (the confrontation scene).

34. Torvald reads a newly delivered letter from Kristine to Nora, learning that Kristine and Nils are leaving, so Nora's crime will not be revealed.

35. Nora announces that despite this good news, she is leaving Torvald and the children.

36. Nora leaves.

Which of these events would you select as the opening of the play?

Ibsen chose a late point of attack, opening the play with event #22! Everything that preceded that event is revealed through exposition.

What is the dramatic question?

In the first scene, the audience is probably asking itself the *McCall's* magazine question: *Can this marriage be saved?* During the second French scene, the audience must wonder about a related question; *Will Nora's secret be revealed?* This second question seems more immediate and urgent than the first, and it drives Nora's actions, but it is subordinate to the first. The pressing dramatic question finally evolves into: *Will the marriage survive Torvald's learning the truth?* While the audience focuses on Torvald's reaction, the dramatic question is actually resolved by Nora's reaction to his reaction.

Is there an obligatory scene?

From the very beginning, the audience shares Nora's dread of what would happen if Torvald discovered her secret. Their confrontation when he does learn that secret is obligatory.

This scene has the play's greatest emotional content. The dramatic question is answered. The audience experiences the resolution of the situation's inherent imbalance (Nora and Torvald's unequal relationship in an untenable marriage).

✔ A sample symbol: Macaroons

Macaroons represent Nora's taste for sweets, which in turn suggests her childlike status. Torvald's forbidding her to have macaroons demonstrates his authoritarianism, and their father-daughter relationship. Nora's secretly buying and hiding macaroons despite his order reveals her deceitfulness, the lack of honesty in their relationship, and her resistance to his control.

✔ The inciting incident

Torvald's imminent promotion to bank manager triggers Nils' demand that Nora protect his job and his threat to reveal Nora's secret. This impending catastrophe breaks the uneasy calm of the marriage.

✔ A sample complication

Nils' decision to leave town with Kristine eliminates his need to keep his bank job and relieves Nora of the threat that her forgery will be revealed, but Nils' letter revealing the secret is already in the mailbox, and only Torvald has the key.

✔ A time lock

Much of the urgency is created by the classic time-lock device. Nils' letter sits in Torvald's mailbox, and it is only a matter of time before he will read it.

✔ Stage actions

Plenty of stage action provides visual interest and energy: Nora and Kristine sew, Nora shows off Christmas presents, Nora offers and hides macaroons, Nora dances, Torvald reads the letters and Dr. Rank's cards, and the children make a brief appearance.

✔ Nora's major objective

At the play's opening, before Nils threatens her, Nora's major objective is to finish paying off the secret loan from Nils. For almost the entire play, Nora's major objective is to prevent Torvald from learning that she criminally forged her father's signature to borrow money to finance their trip to Italy (Torvald thinks that the trip was financed by money Nora inherited from her father). Torvald is an authoritarian prig who fears social disgrace, and whose male pride would be crushed by the news that his cute little wife financed his trip.

Once the major objective is achieved or rendered impossible (in this play, rendered impossible by Torvald's discovery of the secret), the protagonist has a different major objective. In the last scene, Nora's new major objective, a *reversal* of her earlier desire to save the marriage, is to become independent, ending her childlike relationship with Torvald, whom she no longer loves.

✔ Nora's minor objectives

In pursuit of her major objective, Nora pursues many minor objectives, such as saving Nils' job, reclaiming her forgery, distracting Torvald from going to his mailbox, and stealing Nils' letter.

✔ A sample scene: The tension of conflicting objectives

After the Christmas dance, Torvald and Nora return to their home, *with conflicting objectives*. Randy with champagne and the sight of Nora's dancing, Torvald wants to enact a sexual fantasy.

Desperate with fear, Nora wants to get Torvald to go to sleep so that he will not read his mail. (She is apparently unwilling to have sex with him to achieve this.)

The playwright delays resolution of this conflict, increasing the tension of the scene. Both of their objectives are frustrated by *complications*: Kristine is waiting for them, so Torvald is stalled until he can get rid of her. Then Dr. Rank visits, further delaying the moment when Nora, and the audience, will know whether Torvald will read the fatal letter. Finally, Nora and Torvald say good night to each other, each expecting the other to go to bed to sleep – a moment of high tension until Torvald tells her that he will read his mail first.

✔ Torvald's 15 objectives (creating separate beats) in Act III

Torvald's major objective at the beginning of the scene is to have sex with Nora, an objective to which he returns several times after some complications. Soon, his new major objective becomes to prevent her from leaving him. Quite a change! Here are his objectives, in order, along with the event that makes it change:

1. *Prevent Nora from returning to the party, to get her to bed*

   But he sees Kristine.

2. *Get rid of Kristine*

   Kristine leaves.

3. *Get Nora in the mood for sex*

   Dr. Rank interrupts them.

4. *Get rid of Dr. Rank*

   Dr. Rank leaves.

5. *Get the mail from his mailbox*

   He gets the mail.

6. *Get Nora in the mood for sex*

Nora puts him off, and he acquiesces.

7. *Read the mail*

He reads the shocking letter from Nils.

8. *Get Nora's confirmation of the allegations*

She admits the truth.

9. *Get her to admit causing great problems for him*

She admits to being at fault.

10. *Instruct her in his damage control plan*

Kristine's letter arrives: Nils will leave town.

11. *Restore the status quo ante of their marriage*

Nora instead forces him to talk about their marriage

12. *Defend himself from her analysis of the marriage*

Nora announces that she's leaving him.

13. *Persuade Nora not to leave*

She convinces him she will not stay.

14. *Get Nora to agree to future contact*

Nora refuses.

15. *Persuade himself that a miracle might bring her back*

In the course of this act Torvald is alternately exhilarated, irritated, sexually aroused, shocked, angered, indignant, self-pitying, determined, desperate, and despairing.

✔ Nora's four objectives in Act III

Characters do not necessarily change beats at the same time as other characters.

Here are Nora's objectives. When you reread the play, find the intervening incidents that cause each beat change. Find out what Torvald says that finally convinces Nora to leave.

1. Return to the party.

2. Say final goodbyes to Dr. Rank.

3. Hear Torvald's reaction to Nils' letter.

4. Leave Torvald.

INDEX